Experience SEDONA Legends and Legacies

Author, Kate Ruland-Thorne

(Dedication)
**To My
Husband,
Keith**

THORNE
ENTERPRISES
PUBLICATIONS, INC.

CREDITS

Editor Aliza Caillou
Cover Design & Graphics Ron Henry Design
Historical Site Map Reed Thorne
Illustrations Jack Proctor
Chapter One - THE ANCIENT ONES by James Bishop, Jr.
Printer Bertelsmann Industry Services, Penny Hancock
        Sacramento, CA

Fourth Printing, 1999

ISBN #09628329-0-1

1989 Thorne Enterprises
Library of Congress Catalog Card Number: 89-51796

ACKNOWLEDGEMENTS

An author can rarely accept full credit for any written project. Without the numerous special people who gave so untiringly of their time and interest, this book would not have been possible. May I extend my warmest appreciation to Rahim Akbarzadeh at the Special Collections Library at N.A.U. who discovered things for me I would have easily overlooked, Callie Smith of Missouri who drove to libraries and schools to get information on Philip Miller and Gorin, Missouri and asked for nothing in return; my friend and mentor Jim Bishop who agreed to do extensive research for me on THE ANCIENT ONES and then agreed to write it; Bennie Blake whose keen eyes and sharp mind caught embarrassing flaws in my copy; Luiz Schlesinger, my 'photo doctor' who reproduced all of my photographs so beautifully and anticipated needs I had overlooked; Ron Henry who always can be counted on to do an excellent job of layout and design; Della Greenwell and her sister Laura Purtymun McBride who spent countless hours telling me stories of her family, sharing her precious photos, and allowing me to drive her up and down the canyon on more than one occasion to point out historic locations; Lin and Marilyn Miller, who opened their heart and not only shared beautiful insights into the life of Abe Miller, but trusted me for months with 14 precious photo albums; Margaret Wallace and Clara McBride, Sedona and Carl Schnebly's daughters, who wrote letter after letter filled with rich memories of their lives with their parents adding wonderful dimensions to that chapter; Joe and Sharon Beeler, Bob Bradshaw, Nassan Gobran and Tony Staude who were tremendous contributors to the interesting aspects of their stories; to Reed Thorne whose brilliant Experience Sedona map inspired this book; and especially to my patient and dear husband Keith, who ate many frozen dinners while I typed and researched. I love you all.

Sedona Miller, *1890's*

Photo courtesy of Paula Schnebly Hokanson

TABLE OF CONTENTS

INTRODUCTION

Carved by wind, water, and geological upheaval, the lush gorge of Oak Creek Canyon and the red rock spires of Sedona have lured people since pre-historic times. The wind may remember the names of those who came before. We know only of their legends, some of which tell of their origins here. Symbols etched or painted on rock faces near their dwelling sites indicate that this was considered a place of healing and sacred ceremonies . . . where visions were revealed and dreams fulfilled. This remains true for people even today.

One need not be inclined toward metaphysical or spiritual ideology to sense the energy that this area exudes. There is something unusual about this place that goes beyond its physical beauty. Even the visitor for one day will sense it.

Many of those who came to Sedona to stay, admit that here they experienced new beginnings . . . life-altering experiences, inspiration, or the fulfillment of dreams which may have lain dormant for years. From the time of the earliest inhabitants to the present-day citizens, Sedona has been a breeding ground for unusual aspirations and experiences. But in the 1860's and 70's, it also was dangerous. In fact all of Arizona was.

According to the Congress of the United States, Arizona Territory wasn't even fit for statehood until 1912. From 1860 until 1912 our state was accused of "not having a sufficient number of law-abiding inhabitants to dominate those who are not law-abiding," and "the statutes of the territory actually permit gambling establishments and saloons to run night and day and Sundays." We were also criticized for having too many Indians.

Arizona Territory was known as Indian country. For two decades, it was too dangerous a place for settlers . . . the law-abiding kind anyway. It would take General George Crook to change all of that when in 1876, following a long campaign, he finally rounded up the last of the Apaches, forced their surrender and marched them off to the San Carlos Reservation.

Within weeks after their surrender, Sedona's first settler, J.J. Thompson discovered Oak Creek Canyon while out hunting with a friend. Figuring any place in Arizona with water must be valuable, Thompson took squatter's rights to a parcel he called Indian Gardens. It was so named because of the lush crop of squash and beans he found, which had been abandoned by a fleeing band of Apaches. And so it was that Thompson, and those who followed, would help comprise the 'law-abiding citizenry' which the territory so badly needed in order to earn statehood.

For Thompson and his fellow pioneers, Sedona's unique landscape, abundant wildlife and lush vegetation inspired tremendous hopes and dreams. It also required considerable taming. This was a wild, inaccessible land, and only years of arduous effort finally made it accessible and inhabitable.

Like its landscape, Sedona's pioneers were a unique breed of people. Only the dedicated and hard working survived, leaving their mark upon the land. Many with an ability to make their dreams come true have left us with their legacies too, while the colorful lifestyles of others are now woven into our legends.

Not all of their stories are told here, but certainly the most interesting. Each left behind an undeniable legacy for which we are the benefactors. Perhaps their stories will aid others to realize their unfulfilled dreams.

It is with the utmost pleasure that some of Sedona's LEGENDS AND LEGACIES will now unfold.

Kate Ruland-Thorne

Chapter One
THE ANCIENT ONES

t night when the streets of your villages are silent and you think them deserted, they will throng with the returning hosts that once filled them and loved this beautiful land. The White Man will never be alone . . . *Chief Seattle*

By all accounts, the nation's news media have decided to crown Greater Sedona the latest "hotspot" among resorts in the Great Southwest. And indeed, it is quite a story. As if drawn by a powerful magnet, millions of tourists from all over the world are making annual pilgrimages to savour Sedona's remarkable scenery, to enjoy the refreshing clean air and water, to relish the burgeoning arts and crafts community, all in a region J.B. Priestley once described as "not quite of this world."

Sedona's discovery by easterners, Asians and Europeans may be topical news in New York and Boston but to the 17 tribes of native Americans, some 200,000 of them living on 20,000,000 acres in Arizona, Greater Sedona's qualities, and those of the Verde Valley, have been part of their heritage since long before the birth of Christ.

Indeed, the abundant ruins and ancient rock art to be found in many canyons and along creeks and streams in the vicinity tell us that Indians lived, traded and played here for hundreds and thousands of years before the first European arrived with sword, horse and axe.

At the famous Palatki ruin between Sedona and Clarkdale, the figure of Kokopela, the little humpbacked flute player is clearly visible in rock art paintings on the ancient sandstone walls. This Anasazi -- Navajo for "the ancient ones" -- fertility figure is carved into cliffs and painted onto rocks throughout Utah, New Mexico, Colorado and Northern Arizona; indeed throughout the Colorado Plateau.

According to Indian lore, Sedona was a favorite meeting ground for rest and relaxation, the kind of a place where a person "can loaf and invite the soul," in poet Walt Whitman's words.

"Close your eyes and reach back with your imagination 1000 years, 2000 years," suggests Fred Spinks an Indian expert with Sedona's Dorian Tours. "Greater Sedona was a meeting place for Indians from all across the Southwest. Indians splashed in the hot springs up and down Oak Creek and fished for trout with spears. They held religious ceremonies in Boynton Canyon. Historical evidence suggests that it was a healing place for them just as it is for us today."

And just as Sedona today is a major trading crossroads, so it was in prehistory. Shells from the Gulf of California and the Pacific Coast were exchanged for pottery and jewelry. Many of the shells, in turn, were swapped for parrot feathers with traders from what is now called South America.

Imagine the surprise of the early Spanish explorers entering Arizona in the 1530's at being met by people wearing feather head-dresses, strings of beads, earrings and heavy bracelets!

Fray Marcos de Niza wrote in 1539 of the "number of turquoises worn as ornaments by the people. Some had as many as three or four strings of green stones around their necks; others carried them as ear-pendants and in their noses."

Perhaps because of its beauty, Greater Sedona in the earliest days was for Indians a peaceful place. Archaeologists and historians are in agreement that whatever disputes might have been raging between Apaches and Zunis, Hopi or Navajo, they left them behind when they journeyed to Greater Sedona and the Verde Valley for hunting and fishing and practicing their religion.

There is evidence, too, that while they didn't live as richly as modern tourists do during their sojourns, they had some elaborate cookouts and ceremonies. "During a recent excavation for a housing development," recounts Quentin Durrel, a Sedona entrepreneur and Indian expert, "large rectangular barbecue pits were uncovered. Believe it or not, they are commercial-sized."

One reason for Greater Sedona's peaceful prehistory is that Indians have always regarded its environs as sacred and special, in part because certain special spots in the area hold the key to many of their "emergence myths."

At Montezuma's Well south of Sedona on Route I-17, the western Yavapai tell a tale of their emergence from the underworld of the Well and of pueblos deep within, built before Noah's time, which once housed many hundreds of people. They also tell of a huge monster living there, an enormous serpent.

Two hundred feet in diameter, this large limestone sink appears as a small spring-fed lake lying in a deep round cavity atop a hill. Through its ancient outlet flows 500,000 gallons of fresh, clear water daily.

Seven-hundred years before Columbus ventured onto our shores, the area surrounding Montezuma's Well was inhabited permanently by the Hohokam. Expert canal-builders and desert farmers from the south, the Hohokam dug more that a mile of irrigation ditches from the Well's outlet to some sixty acres of garden plots.

In the twelfth century, the Hohokams were joined by the Sinaguan people from Arizona's northern plateau region. Between 1300 and 1400 A.D., they drew together more closely in their pit houses for greater security, preparing for some destructive event - or a series of them. True to prophecy, those events did occur, causing them to abandon the Verde Valley in the 1400's, leaving behind great Pueblos like Tuzigoot in Clarkdale and an estimated 60,000 ruins in the lush area between the Verde River and Flagstaff.

Home to hundreds of Sinaguans, Tuzigoot, when excavated in 1933 and 1934, was found to contain 92 rooms, larger than any Sedona hotel today. Corpses of their little children had been buried beneath living-room floors, perhaps in hopes that their spirits would be reborn. Of Tuzigoot's 170 burials, 42 percent were of infants and children younger than eight years of age. Twenty-nine percent were adults, 21-45. Only four-and-one-half percent were people over 45.

To this day, scientists are perplexed about the reasons for the "great abandonment." It remains one of the most enduring mysteries in the history of the Southwest. "Why should an area as bountiful as the Verde ever have been abandoned?" asks Peter Pilles, chief archaeologist for the Coconino National Forest. "Yet their sophisticated cultural system, the culmination of six hundred years of development, collapsed a mere century before the Spanish entered Arizona."

Down through the centuries, many bands of different Indians came and went through Sedona's Oak Creek Canyon and the Verde Valley. Indeed some historians contend that the Hopi, now living on their fabled Mesas to the north and east of Sedona, may have had their origins in the Verde Valley.

According to Hopi legend, the first Hopi people emerged from a great hole in the earth. The first world of the Hopi was a bad place, so their emergence story goes. Then the god who made the world said he would make a second world. He told Spider Woman that she should lead the people up to the second world.

Spider Woman showed them the way and when they got there they began planting and building homes. For some reason, however, there was a great deal of killing and the situation in general was no better than it had been in the first world. Besides the killing, there was no game to hunt.

Once again the early Hopi appealed to Spider Woman. She went to the god and told him of their plight. He said he would make a third world and that Spider Woman should lead the people again.

In the third world there was no killing, and for a few years there was plenty of game. But when the people tried to plant food, the plants wouldn't grow because there wasn't enough light or heat.

The god then told Spider Woman to build bonfires around the fields of maize and beans. That worked for a time and plants began to grow but the world was too dark, and people were dying in large numbers. Again Spider Woman went to tell the god what was happening to the first Hopis.

Somewhat annoyed by this time, god said he would make the fourth world, but it would be the very last one he would ever make. That is how it came about that the Hopi people began a long journey to their present Mesas.

It took them a long time to get there, but at last they came into the light and they found good land to plant. That was thousands of years ago, and they have remained there ever since. In fact, one of the Hopi villages, Old Oraibi, is regarded as the oldest continuously inhabited settlement in the United States.

For nearly a century, archaeologists have been trying to determine when the Hopi came to their Mesas and from where. With each passing year, the case grows stronger that they came from "Palatkwapi" -- "Place of the Red Rocks" known today as Sedona.

Writing in Plateau Magazine, which is published by the Museum of Northern Arizona at Flagstaff, James Byrkit asserts that "as time went by, a number of clans including the Rain Cloud, the Water, the Young Corn and the Rabbit Brush, built Palatkwapi into a great cultural and religious center. They were blessed with the assistance of a host of guardian spirits -- including Eototo, the deity of the Bear clan, a chief of the Kachinas."

When the deities told the Palatkwapi people that they were destined to migrate to new locations, the early Hopi disobeyed, preferring to enjoy the warm fertile region, so blessed with abundant springs and streams. Eventually, with so much leisure time they became self-indulgent, Byrkit postulates.

After more time passed, even the priests forgot their responsibilities and joined their followers in the pursuit of pleasure. But it all came to an end when the few remaining virtuous Hopi leaders beseeched their gods to visit upon them a great flood to punish the pleasure-driven inhabitants.

Soon great towering clouds gathered, and falling heavier and heavier, a great rain began to come down. It was a truly great flood and it forced the Palatkwapi to abandon their villages and homes and escape to higher ground.

Thereupon the Hopi began a slow northeastward migration, constructing a series of pueblos along the way so that they could rest and grow their blue corn. It is said that they settled at a place called Kwitsalvi for some years. Years later, at one pueblo, Homolovi, swarms of insects appeared out of nowhere and began to attack the babies, bringing much suffering.

According to Byrkit's fascinating account, the refugees moved on again, finally coming to the village of Walpi, on the First Mesa, where they were met by the Snake Chief. He asked them from

whence they had come and whether they wanted to live at Walpi.

Naturally, the refugees were tired of fleeing, first the flood that had nearly drowned them all at "the place of the Red Rocks," then the insects so they agreed to try to earn the acceptance of the Snake Chief. The Chief of the Water Clan made rain one afternoon and that was all it took for the Palatkwapi people to be asked to live there permanently. Here, at last, they managed to return to their old temperate, disciplined and responsible ways.

Traveling to those haunted Mesas today, a visitor can see their descendants farming, dancing and making pottery. Sadly, however, writes Byrkit, "no one remains who can speak knowingly of the Palatkwapi."

Venturing deeper into Greater Sedona's past, scientists believe the first measurable human presence occurred sometime around 8000 B.C. A great variety of projectile points have been excavated indicating that the first inhabitants did their best in hunting the camels, elephants and sabre-tooth tigers that roamed the Verde Valley in those days.

Small animal figures, 3,000 to 4,000 years old, made of split willow twigs have been found in a Sycamore Canyon cave near Clarkdale, according to archaeologist Peter Pilles, Jr. "Identical figures," he reports, "have been found in the Grand Canyon suggesting these were magical talismans used to ensure a successful hunt."

These first inhabitants of the so-called Dry Creek Phase (8000 B.C. - A.D.   roamed around in bands, along the tributaries of Oak Creek, Dry Creek, Beaver Creek until the beginnings of agriculture around the time of the birth of Christ. Then came the construction of the first pit houses scattered in villages in the uplands and, according to Pilles, along the foothills of the Mogollon Rim.

Excavations suggest that these first homes were rectangular in shape, with rounded ends and with fire pits and storage places dug into the floors. "Dwellings were generally small," Pilles asserts, "suggesting occupation by a single family."

How do modern-day archaeologists know that the first inhabitants made the shift from hunting to agriculture? Simply put, they have been utilizing the same technique future scientists will employ when they try to ascertain what kind of people lived in Sedona in the late 1980's -- they went through their garbage and learned that the rocks they used for preparing food had changed -- from those used to grind seeds and nuts to larger, rectangular ones, ideal for grinding corn.

It was soon after the beginning of the first century that pottery was introduced into the Verde Valley, indicating contact with the Anasazi living in the high deserts along the Little Colorado River, as well as the Hohokam to the south.

By 700 A.D., these Southern Sinaguans were joined by a people called Hakataya from the uplands and, so Pilles's interpretation goes, by groups of Hohokam from the Phoenix-Salt River Valley who established their irrigation-based agricultural technology.

There was great prosperity during this period due to the lush farming opportunities and the fact that small groups of Indians came into the Valley to obtain salt, argillite and copper for trade.

By 800 A.D., these Sinaguans began to build circular, deeper houses, indicating hefty increases in the population and a more sophisticated social organization. Researchers today marvel at just how sophisticated these early inhabitants were, with their mastery of dry-farming devices such as terraces, rock-cleared areas and rock-outlined field borders that resembled checkerboards. Evidently they maximized the growing potential of the land by outlining farm plots with stones or laying them out near large boulders.

It is easy to imagine great celebrations along the banks of Oak Creek almost 1100 years ago near where L'Auberge de Sedona is today. Besides corn, there would have been nuts (sweet acorn, pinon, and walnuts), seeds (sunflower, goldeneye, wild grasses), and berries (manzanita, juniper, cedar, mulberry, hackberry, lemon berries) and the ripening fruit of the treasured banana yucca.

Cooking techniques included boiling in pots over a fire along the creeks or stone-building, in which heated stones were dropped into a cooking vessel. Some foods were also roasted and parched with hot coals in baskets. In the spring, leafy greens were collected and boiled (chenopod and amaranth). In mid-summer the desert fruits and seeds, mainly mesquite, cacti, and paloverde became ripe. Saguaro fruits were picked with a stick consisting of two long saguaro ribs tied together with a wooden hook at the end. The fruits were eaten raw as they were picked or mixed with water for juice. The seeds were washed, fried and ground for immediate consumption or storage.

Some food was available all year-round, especially the agave which ripened in higher elevations and provided a staple food - mescal - that could be relied upon in times of need.

The way the early ones prepared the agave is sophisticated even by today's standards. The base was dug out and the sharp ends of the leaves cut off. The hearts were cooked in large roasting pits for several days. As with most other foods, mescal was either eaten after being cooked or dried and stored for future use; it was usually eaten in combination with other foods. As much as three to four months might be spent in one area preparing mescal, and large stands of agave were points where local bands came together.

Men and boys did essentially all the bow-and-arrow hunting of large game, such as bear, and small birds, particularly quail, as well as hunting down smaller animals with a throwing stick. Deer were driven into blinds by several men hunting together, or stalked at close range by individual hunters camouflaged with deer-head masks.

Like the plains indians with the buffalo, the Sinaguans, and the

Montezuma's Castle (left) and Tuzigoot (right) *were built by the Sinagua people around 1100 A.D. and were abandoned mysteriously after 1400 A.D. These people are believed to be related to the modern day Hopi.*

Yavapai who came later, utilized almost every part of a deer for food, clothing or tools. It was their way of paying respect to the dead animal. Meantime, baited traps and snares were used to catch coyotes, wildcats and foxes. Women, too, would join the men in animal drives for rabbits and antelope. But those were special occasions. All year-round families collected lizards, locusts, grasshoppers and caterpillars for food.

All the while trade was blooming according to Pilles. "It was a very well organized activity at this time, with Verde craftsmen manufacturing ornaments of local materials, presumably destined for the Hohokam market to the south," he relates. "Evidence for such activity has been found at Perkinsville -- raw argillite stone-working tools, and Hohokam-style argillite ornaments in various stages of completion in a Sinaguan-style pit house."

Between 1000 and 1125 A.D. population density increased and many of the new pit houses began to be made of masonry. Also, Anasazi ceramics from the north were in widespread use in these larger houses. Peace reigned throughout this period, and commercial trading activity flourished, recent excavations suggest.

Then began the so-called Honanki phase which lasted until 1300 A.D. It was during this time that the earliest room blocks at Tuzigoot and Montezuma Castle were constructed. Other new settlements used elevated places overlooking waterways and floodplains, such as early parts of Clear Creek Ruins and the Cornville Ruins Groups.

Montezuma's Well, *This was a gathering place down through the ages for sacred ceremonies among various ancient people and is the place of origin for the Western Yavapai "emergence myth."*

Photos by Kate Ruland-Thorne

During this period, there was a major acceleration in the construction of cliff dwellings in the Red Rock country near Sedona. Honanki, which gives this phase its name, and neighboring Palatki are two of the largest and best preserved cliff dwellings in the Verde Valley. They were first described for a large audience by Jesse Walter Fewkes in 1895 on his way up the Verde Valley to the Hopi Mesas. Tree-ring dating indicates a building stage in 1271, although actual occupation probably spans many years on either side of that date. Due to the work of the Coconino National Forest staff, principally Pete Pilles as well as Time Expeditions, these ruins have been stabilized and interpretative programs have been developed.

At this writing, Time Expeditions in Sedona, under license with the Forest Service, runs daily tours to Honanki near Boynton Canyon. At Palatki further to the west, Pilles has been spearheading a cleanup crew to remove much of the modern graffiti which mars the walls of the ruin. In the process, many early pictographs have been revealed.

The Honanki Phase gave way to what scientists call the Tuzigoot Phase which lasted from 1300 A.D. until about 1400. It was during this phase that the first indications of political control are visible to 20th century experts. The main clue is that the pueblos were built about two miles apart.

The Beaver Creek series begins in the uplands not far from route I-17 where the canyon first opens as it winds its way through the

Mogollon rim. In this small valley is a pueblo with its forty-one rooms arranged around a central plaza. About two miles downstream lies Sacred Mountain, an isolated white limestone butte. On top are three blocks of forty rooms that outline a plaza. Here are a series of large terraces which might have been work areas.

Pilles and others tell us that the two large pueblos at Montezuma Well form the next link in the chain. Their location indicates the control these early ones had over their water supplies. The next pueblo, today located in Montezuma Estates, resembles a miniature Tuzigoot, being a small hill covered with ruins. The last in the series is Montezuma Castle itself.

When the Spanish entered the valley in 1583 bringing the first horses, they encountered only a smattering of Indians. A hundred years earlier, a culture that was becoming sophisticated and even elaborate had simply disappeared.

Did they all die? Did they migrate to the west, to the north? "The reasons are unknown," says Pilles. "We still have much to learn."

For the next several hundred years, the Spaniards Antonio de Espejo, Marcos Farfan, and Juan de Onate travelled up and down the Verde Valley looking for gold, finding nothing but salt and copper and leaving legends in their wake. Historical documents indicate that the numbers of Yavapai -- for which one of the two counties surrounding Sedona is named -- began congretating in the region, along with the Apache and also some Navajo who are Apache cousins who'd migrated down from Canada.

Who were the Yavapai, descendents of the Anasazi, the Sinagua or the Hopi? No scientist will say for sure.

What is known is that there were many similarities in the culture of the Yavapai and the Apache, a fact which contributed to a great deal of misunderstanding through the years about the ethnic identity of the two peoples.

To the U.S. Cavalry, they were one and the same, as a host of massacres in the 19th century demonstrated.

Until the 1860's, when gold was finally discovered in central Arizona, it is believed that there was little contact between these Yavapai/Apache and Whites. Unlike the Apache, the Yavapai avoided fights when they could, but they were under great pressure from the settlers and were constantly being moved around by the Cavalry. If their days of freedom seemed numbered, it is because they were.

On November 9, 1871, an executive order approved the creation of the Rio Verde Reservation located in the Middle Verde Valley. On December 21, Gen. George Crook ordered that all "roving Apache" were to be on this reservation by February 15, 1872, or be treated as hostile.

In the course of forcing the Yavapai and Apache onto the reservation, the U.S. Army wiped out a large band of them in the Salt River Canyon on December 27, 1872. The Indians were slaughtered by soldiers who shot blindly into a cave in which they had taken

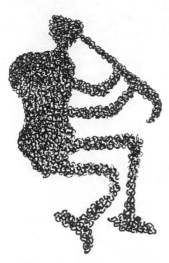

Kokopela *the hump-backed flute player is a fertility symbol which was used by most pueblo societies throughout the Southwest.*

Honanki and Palatki, *discovered by Jesse W. Fewkes in 1895, are two more examples of the large and well-preserved Sinagua cliff dwellings which exist throughout the Sedona and Verde Valley area. Tree ring dating indicates they were built around 1271 A.D. Photos by Michael Peach*

refuge. Of all the massacres during the 1860's and 1870's -- at Bloody Basin, Skull Valley and Date Creek -- the one at "Skeleton Cave" is still remembered as one of the most horrendous in Yavapai history because of the blind killing.

By 1873, most Yavapai had been rounded up and marched onto the Rio Verde Reservation near what is now Camp Verde just off Route I-17, south of Sedona. Despite various epidemics and adversities, these Yavapai, principally by means of their own aboriginal tools, managed to dig an irrigation ditch and produce many successful harvests. But it was not to last.

In the mid-1870's, a group of contractors from Tucson who sold goods to various Indian reservations became alarmed at the Yavapais' growing self-sufficiency. So they lobbied hard for a new government executive order to officially transfer the Yavapai onto the Apache Reservation at San Carlos. General Crook protested the move but to no avail. But he did promise the Yavapai that he would make sure they would be allowed to return to their homelands and receive their own reservation once they had learned the "White people's ways" and shown their loyalty as army scouts.

History tells us that relocation to San Carlos took the form of a forced march in 1875 over 181 miles of wretched terrain in the dead of winter. More that 100 indians were never to see Greater Sedona, the Red Rocks or the Verde River again; they froze to death before the band reached their destination. Some did manage to escape the Cavalry but only a mere handful.

At San Carlos, the Yavapais were settled in an area separate from the Apaches, although they were friendly and even engaged in intermarriage, but they weren't to remain there for long either. Farming was difficult because of the lack of a decent irrigation system and the natives had to revert back to their ancient hunting and gathering ways.

In the late 1880's and early 1890's, the Indian Agents at San Carlos decided to violate the relocation executive order and quietly began to encourage the Yavapai and Apache to return home to their lands near Sedona. Lest anyone think otherwise, the agents were not acting out of compassion. Their land at San Carlos, including the so-called "Mineral Strip," was then free for leasing to non-Indian interests.

Many Yavapais did return to their home areas and hacked out a living working on farms, ranches, road construction, or anywhere they could earn a living. Some rented small sections of land from white farmers. But they had lost their land forever, and their ancient way of life had evanesced into the cosmos.

By 1912, there were so many Yavapais working in the copper mines and at the smelter at Clarkdale, 15 miles southwest of Sedona, that the Bureau of Indian Affairs in Washington D.C. opened a day school for them. After World War 1, when a series of bloody strikes smashed the power of the mine unions, many new jobs opened up for the Yavapai. In 1914 and again in 1916, an additional 448 acres with water rights were set up for the Yavapai eight miles west of Camp Verde at Middle Verde. This created a resurgence in farming and contributed to a modest return to self-sufficiency.

The slowdown and finally closure of the mines in north and central Arizona during the 1930's and 1940's proved to be another heavy blow to the Yavapais. Consequently, more of them returned to reservations.

In 1969, 60 acres near the former mining community of Clarkdale were established as reservation land for them. A Department of Housing and Urban Development program helped to provide new homes.

Today, a Yavapai tribal project is visible to tourists, a tourist center complex associated with the Montezuma Castle National Monument. But otherwise the Indians who once worked, played and prayed here have become all but invisible, the victims not of Spanish lust for gold, or their own warfare, but a bizarre combination of the known and the unknown.

The secret of the "Great Abandonment" of the 1400's may never be known; was it disease, famine, a supernatural event? However the "known factor" that brought the seeds of death and destruction to well over half of the Indian population of Arizona -- and an end to the world they had known since the dawn of their history -- is abundantly clear to experts like Boye De Mente, author of the Visitor's Guide to Arizona's Indian Reservations.

"It was the American beaver trappers," he writes, "the so called Mountain Men who began appearing on the rivers of northern and central Arizona in the 1820's. This led to a gradual confiscation of Indian lands and the removal of Indian populations by an extraordinary cultural arrogance translated as 'the right of discovery', a policy spelled out in a Supreme Court decision in 1823."

This decision held that the discovery of the American continent "gave" them the exclusive right to extinguish the Indian title of occupancy, either by purchase or conquest. The decision went on to say that this right took precedence over all other rights, and that the U.S. Government alone could hold title to any and all lands claimed by Indians. As a final clincher, the decision ruled that Indians were to be considered as mere "occupants" of the lands they lived on, and while they were to be "protected" as long as they were peaceful, it was specifically spelled out that they were "incapable of transfering title of their lands to others."

Beginning in the 1960's, Arizona has witnessed a renaissance of the Red Man, once on the verge of suffering the same fate as the Mohawks, the Powhattan, the Seneca and dozens of other tribes, and the buffalo. Today, Arizona is still Indian country.

The Navajo, Hopi, Apache, Papago and Pima-Maricopa have moved back from the abyss to the beginning of a recovery. Because they own 28 percent of the land, by default they will become the landed agricultural gentry of the state by the 21st century, so rapidly are developers chewing up white-owned farms.

Such is not to be the fate of the Anasazi or the Sinagua or the other mysterious peoples who once lived here. But they have left something powerful behind as a legacy. One has only to have a curiosity and an imagination to appreciate it.

To hikers in Sycamore Canyon and Beaver Creek, to canoeists on the Verde River, artists sketching at Red Rock Crossing or campers in Oak Creek Canyon, there comes a great silence at twilight.

Listen!
Can you hear them?

Chapter Two
SEDONA'S FAMILIES OF FIRSTS
The Thompsons, James,
Howards and Purtymuns

hen John James (J.J.) Thompson ran away from home at the age of eleven, he never looked back. The year was approximately 1853 and home was Londonderry, Ireland.

"I got tired of goin' to school six days a week and spendin' Sunday in church," was the reason he later gave for leaving.

A typical eleven year-old run-away without any means of support would not have made it very far, but this was no ordinary youngster. Before the year was out, J.J. Thompson had found his way across the Atlantic ocean to America. It was this same kind of pluck and determination which eventually brought him to his final home on the banks of Oak Creek in Arizona.

The estimated year of Jim Thompson's birth was 1842. He spoke very little about his family or his early life in Ireland. We can only imagine how, when he ran away, he first managed to get across the Irish sea to the great port of Liverpool, England, where ships bound for America set sail several times a day.

America, that was where he wanted to go, but no one allowed a child to travel alone, even if the child had the money to pay for his passage. Of course J.J. Thompson had no money at all.

The story goes that J.J. hung around the Liverpool docks for several days until luck smiled upon him in the form of another young man in his twenties. This man took pity on the young lad and offered to pay J.J.'s passage and assume guardianship for him until they reached New York. Then Thompson would be on his own again.

After arriving in New York, the fabled luck of the Irish smiled upon him once more. Young Thompson met another lad, this one closer to his own age, whose father was a ship captain bound for Galveston, Texas. Thompson's new-found friend assured him that once in Texas, the two could probably get jobs fighting the Comanche. It was an irresistible offer.

Once in Galveston, however, young Thompson's friend was forced to bid him goodbye, probably because his father did not

15

approve of their plans to fight the Indians. So Thompson was left to find his own way again.

This time, he met a man named Finley who took the boy home with him to Refugio, Texas where he was raised as the Finley couple's only child. When Texas seceded from the Union in 1861, Thompson had just turned 19. He enlisted in the Southern Army and during the four years of the Civil War, he spent part of his time in a prison camp in Illinois and his last year in a Georgia hospital with a musket ball wound in his arm and shoulder.

At war's end, J.J. returned to his home in Refugio long enough to visit his adoptive parents, then bid them goodbye once more. This time his adventurous spirit led him into Mexico where he worked for a company trying to raise cotton, and later on a ranch learning to be a cowboy. Once back in Refugio, he took a job as trail boss on a cattle drive to California.

The year was approximately 1868 when Thompson left Texas for California. He was 26 years old. The cattle company never did reach California. In Utah, the herd was sold to the Mormons, and J.J. took his pay and headed for the 'gold fields' on the Colorado River. He had fallen for the tales of gold nuggets that could be picked up like apples along the mighty river's banks near the foot of the Grand Canyon. It was an adventure that ended in disappointment, but it did get him into Arizona Territory.

Thompson rode his horse over a hundred miles of mountain and canyon to the northern-most finger of the Colorado River, stopping near the present-day Lake Mead. Here he either built or bought a raft and went into the ferry business on the Colorado River. During that time, he lived with the Abraham James family. Abraham James had left Missouri in 1869 bound for the California gold fields. With him were his wife, Elizabeth, seven children and a small herd of cattle.

After a few years in California, the discouraged family headed back east again, but encountered poison water in the Nevada desert. Here they lost most of their stock. They were forced to abandon their wagons and after much suffering from thirst, arrived on the Muddy River in southern Nevada.

When Abraham and his sons returned several weeks later to retrieve their wagons, they found they had been robbed of everything of value. Abraham rented a farm on the Muddy River and spent the next few years rebuilding his livestock herds.

The James family's daughter, Margrett Parlee, was only six years old when the dashing young J.J. Thompson started boarding with her family on the Muddy River. She was twelve when J.J. sold his ferry to a Swiss fellow named Bonelli and headed for Arizona Territory. By that time J.J. Thompson and Abraham James were the best of friends and the pretty young Margrett James had already caught J.J.'s eye.

With the money from the sale of his ferry business to Bonelli in 1875, Thompson purchased two wagons and eight pair of oxen. He loaded the wagons with rock salt which he dug from a cliff near the Colorado River and took it to the salt-hungry frontier town of Prescott in Arizona Territory. In those days, salt was used for meat preservation as well as for a condiment, and Prescott's Fort Whipple Army Post was happy to buy most of Thompson's salt.

This time, the enterprising Thompson purchased wood shingles with the money from the sale of his salt and loaded his wagons again for a trip to Phoenix in the hopes of another successful sale. However, things did not go as well this time.

Phoenix, in the 1870's, was only a grouping of adobe structures, and shingles were not used for adobe roofs.

Undeterred, Thompson simply stored the unwanted shingles, butchered one of his oxen, made jerky and sold enough of it to pay his way back to Prescott. Once there, he sold his wagons and teams, used the money to outfit a horse and a pack mule and headed into the Verde Valley to find a place to settle down.

For the first year, Thompson farmed with a friend, Ed Conway, at a place near the present Page Springs. Then one day while hunting with another friend, B.F. Copple, discovered the lush, wild canyon of Oak Creek. The two arrived there just weeks after General Crook's famed army scout, Al Seiber, had routed out the last of the Apaches living in the canyon.

Determining that any place in Arizona with water was a desirable place to settle, Thompson took 'Squatter's Rights' to Indian Gardens in Oak Creek Canyon. The year was 1876, and Thompson's land was located on the opposite side of the road where the present Indian Gardens store now stands. He named his place Indian Gardens because he found a well-tended garden of squash, beans and corn, suddenly abandoned by a family of Apaches who had been marched off to the San Carlos reservation. Thompson would become the first white man to settle in Oak Creek Canyon.

Thompson built a cabin on the land and continued to expand his farm. He also wrote his Nevada friends, the James family, encouraging them to join him.

Abraham James heeded the call. He loaded up his family and all their possessions and livestock and arrived in the Verde Valley in 1878. The James family settled first near Page Springs, and J.J. Thompson began to court 14 year-old Margrett James. By the time Margrett and J.J. married in 1880, the James family had moved to land just below the present King's Ransom Motel off Hwy. 179, known today as Copper Cliffs. They built Sedona's first irrigation ditch and rightfully became Sedona's first settlers.

When Margrett Parlee James married J.J. Thompson, she was sixteen years old and he was 38. Because Thompson's farm in the canyon was too remote and difficult to get to, Thompson built a cabin for his bride on land where the Sedona Arts Center stands today.

In 1882, J.F. (Frank) Thompson was born to Margrett and J.J. in their cabin with Grandma (Elizabeth) James attending as midwife. Thereafter Frank Thompson was acknowledged as the first white child to be born in what was to become the city of Sedona.

The Thompson family eventually grew to include seven boys and two girls. Their second child, Lizzie, was born in 1884. Neither Frank, Lizzie nor the other Thompson children would ever know their grandfather Abraham because he had died in 1881.

After Abraham James and his family settled in Sedona, they always moved in the summer months with their cattle to a canyon north of Mund's Park near Flagstaff. The canyon would become known as James Canyon. In the summer of 1881, just before his grandson Frank Thompson was born, Abraham was caught in a severe summer rainstorm, became soaked and died of pneumonia shortly afterwards.

Although Abraham James lived in Sedona for only two years, he was responsible for giving many of the red rock formations their landmark names. Just one of James' names was ever changed. The original name Abraham James christened Cathedral Rock was 'Courthouse Butte.' To this day, old-timers are still furious that someone down through the years changed its name to Cathedral.

Ten years after her husband's death, Elizabeth James married Old Bear Howard when she was 63 and he was 77. The marriage lasted three months. (See story on Bear Howard for details). In 1896, Elizabeth abandoned her Sedona property and moved to the Red Rock Crossing area (known then as Red Rock). She also lived for awhile at Indian Gardens and finally moved to Price, Utah where she died in 1905 at the home of her oldest daughter, Louisa.

In the meantime, J.J Thompson struggled hard and long just to make a living for his burgeoning family. He would pack a muleload of trout that he'd caught in Oak Creek and sell it to the troops stationed at Camp Verde. Often the army camp gave him contracts to bring hay or firewood to their camp as well. After the mines opened in Jerome, Thompson hauled freight both to the mines and later to Flagstaff when tracks were being laid for the Santa Fe Railroad through Northern Arizona. All of this activity didn't allow time to tend his farm at Indian Gardens, so Thompson hired an old Arkansas bear hunter, Richard Wilson, to help out with the chores.

In 1885, Thompson was called to Prescott on business and asked old Wilson to come down from the canyon each night after tending the Indian Gardens farm and look after his young family while he was away. It was summer and Grandma James was away with her cattle.

The first night after Thompson left, Wilson failed to show up. For eight days Margrett Thompson and her two small children remained alone. Margrett knew Wilson to be a man of his word and soon became worried that he was either sick or dead.

On the ninth day, two men rode up to the Thompson home. They were friends, Judge John Goodwin and his son Tom, from Jerome. They came to fetch the key to the Thompson cabin at Indian Gardens because they had been invited by Thompson to stay there and fish. Margrett was relieved to see them. She told them that old Wilson had the key and she was sure something terrible had happened to him. The men said they would look for him.

The Thompsons were aware that Wilson had seen tracks of a monstrous grizzly bear between Indian Gardens and Sedona and they knew Wilson was obsessed with finding that bear. Before J.J left for Prescott, Wilson had given him his large caliber bear gun to take to Prescott for repairs. That meant Wilson had only a small rifle with him when he headed toward the Thompson home nine days earlier.

Before the present road through Oak Creek Canyon existed, the only way to get through the canyon was over a rough trail at the foot of Steamboat Rock by way of what is today called Wilson Mountain. This mountain was so named because of what these searchers were about to discover.

It began with the sound of a dog barking. The Goodwins slapped the reins against their horses and urged them to hurry up the steep canyon toward the direction of the noise.

In the big box canyon that now can be crossed by Midgley Bridge, they found the body of Richard Wilson. His faithful dog was standing nearby. Wilson's face was down in a stream, and when they turned him over they discovered he had little face left. It had been either bitten or torn off by a bear. A Coroner's inquest was held at the scene of the killing a few days later, and this was the story which was pieced together:

Apparently old Wilson had gotten as far as the box canyon when he spied fresh tracks of the big grizzly he'd been looking for. Wilson had been hunting grizzly for so long, he had no fear of them. The fact that he had only a small rifle and an untrained hound along did not deter him in the least. He followed the tracks up a brushy canyon, spotted the bear and shot it. But the bear was only wounded. Foolishly, Wilson continued after the bear and just as he stepped passed a stand of Arizona Cypress, the bear leaped out at him, catching him by surprise. Wilson dropped his rifle and ran for a tree. He tried to climb the tree, but the bear caught him by the heel of his hob-nail boot and pulled him down. One of the boots was found near the tree with the marks of bear teeth in it. The Cypress tree which Wilson had tried to climb had a thick limb, almost twisted off, which showed how desperately the old hunter had tried to hang on.

Fifteen feet from the tree was the stream where Wilson gasped his last breath, apparently crawling there to get a drink after the deadly blow from the bear. The Coroner gave the cause of death as drowning.

Wilson's body was so decomposed by the time it was discovered that he was buried on the spot in a shallow grave beneath a pile of rocks. The bed rock near the surface didn't allow them to dig a deeper grave. At the base of the cliff where Wilson was buried his friends carved the initials R.W. into the rock. Some years later, Wilson's bones were dug up and re-buried at Indian Gardens.

Fifteen years later, Jim Thompson's son Frank who was only three years old when the incident took place, found the skeleton of a huge bear two miles from the scene of the killing. He brought the skull home, and his father asked him if he'd also found old Wilson's hunting knife. It was looked for but never found. J.J. Thompson always believed that Wilson stabbed the bear with his big knife just before he died and the bear carried it off before succumbing to its own deadly wound.

Two years after Richard Wilson was killed by a bear, the Thompson's third child and only other daughter, Clara, was born in 1887. Before Clara was one year old, J.J. moved his family to his farm at Indian Gardens after managing to build a rough wagon road up the stream bed from Sedona to Indian Gardens. That road was washed out by a flood the following winter, so J.J. built his next road around Steamboat Rock near Midgley Bridge and up Wilson Canyon. From there, the family had to unload their wagons onto pack horses in order to continue the rest of the way to Indian Gardens.

When J.J's boys were older, they worked together to complete the wagon road from Wilson Canyon to Indian Gardens by 1905 using picks, shovels and dynamite. The wagon road from Indian Gardens through Oak Creek Canyon was not opened until 1914. It was completed by others.

Nevertheless, these were J.J. Thompson's road building years and the fact that he was in his mid-sixties didn't slow him down. The Schnebly Hill Road from Sedona to Flagstaff was another Thompson project, which he and his crew began in 1901 and completed 1902. Coconino County paid J.J. $600 for his efforts, although other old-timers had been hacking away at that same road since 1896.

Between 1890 and 1911, six more sons were born to Margrett and J.J. Thompson: Fred, Charley, Jimmie, Albert, Washington and Guy. The seven Thompson boys were always referred to as 'the boys,' and Margrett Thompson was the kind of mother who believed fervently that her 'boys' could do no wrong.

By 1887, Bear Howard, his daughter, Mattie, her husband, Steve Purtymun, and their six sons and two daughters were living in the canyon. The Thompsons and the Purtymuns decided that between the two familys, there was need for a school. So halfway between the Purtymans' ranch near Junipine and the Thompsons' ranch at Indian Gardens, the first old log schoolhouse was built in 1899 on a flat above the creek in a place now called Lower Manzanita

The Thompson Clan, 1905
The J.J. Thompson family in front of their log cabin home at Indian Gardens. (back row) Lizzie Thompson Purtymun, Frank, Clara Thompson and Fred. (seated) Maggie and Jim Thompson, W.G. Green is leaning on his mother. Jimmy and Charley Thompson are on their knees in front and Albert is sitting on the ground. Photo courtesy of Laura Purtymun McBride

First Homestead at Indian Gardens, 1876 *J.J. Thompson's original cabins were built on the east side of Oak Creek. Wilson Mountain is in the background. Photo courtesy of Laura Purtymun McBride*

Grandma Thompson, 1913 *She holds her last child, Guy, born at Indian Gardens in 1911. Photo courtesy of Laura Purtymun McBride*

21

Campground. It was a summer school only. The first teacher was (D.E.) Ellsworth Schnebly, brother-in-law to Sedona Miller Schnebly for whom the town soon would be named. The only students in the school were the Thompson and Purtymun children, with one exception, Bessie Thomas.

All the desks in the little log schoolhouse were homemade by the two families. The schoolhouse was heated by a big wood-burning stove in the colder months, and the children took turns keeping the fire burning.

There is a flat area of ground called 'Fightin Flat' not far from where the old schoolhouse stood. It was so named because two of the Purtymun boys, Charley and Dan, always got into a fight there on their way home from school. Their little sister Ida was the cause of it all.

The boys had spoiled Ida after she was born by carrying her around all the time. A family saying was that Ida didn't develop legs until she was ten because her brothers wouldn't let her walk. By the time Ida was old enough to go to school, her brothers had tired of carrying her. Apparently they didn't have the heart to tell her no when she demanded to be carried home from school, so they simply fought it out each day in order to determine who would carry Ida home.

The walk to and from school was three miles each way. The children often crossed the creek several times, and on numerous occasions, they would see fresh bear tracks. Looking out for bears was a constant concern for the children, who all were aware of the terrible death of Richard Wilson.

One day when Clara and Lizzie Thompson set out to find a lost calf near Mund's Springs, they ran right into a bear. They were so terrified, they started running around the hillside, only to meet head-on with the same bear again. By the time the girls got home, their arms and legs were bloody and their clothes were nearly torn off from fleeing from that bear.

Lizzie and Clara Thompson, Margrett and J.J.'s only daughters, one day would marry two of the Purtymun boys, Jess and Albert. By combining the two families, the infamous old Bear Howard became grandpa to their descendants.

Clara Thompson had just turned 16 when she married Albert Purtymun, age 22, on July 1, 1903. The occasion was cause for a great celebration. J.J. brought a load of lumber from Flagstaff to build a dance floor. The wedding took place at the Thompson home in Indian Gardens. All the Thompson and Purtymun boys helped bring the load of lumber down the steep slope called 'Thompson's Ladder.' They achieved this by nailing six planks together, putting a chain at one end and hitching a horse to it.

Everyone from miles around was invited to the wedding. The celebration lasted three days and three nights. J.J. Thompson had such a good time that he wouldn't allow anyone to fall asleep. When

Sedona's First School, 1897 *The first school in Oak Creek Canyon was located on 'School House Flat'. It was built here because of its location half-way between the homes of the Purtymuns and Thompsons whose children attended. It closed in 1901 when the Purtymun family moved away. Photo courtesy of Laura Purtymun McBride*

SOUVENIR

School District No. 4
OAK CREEK, COCONINO CO., ARIZ.

1901

Presented By
D. E. Schnebly, *Teacher*

SCHOOL BOARD

Mrs. M. E. Purtymun
Mrs. J. J. Thompson
N. G. Layton, Co. Sup't

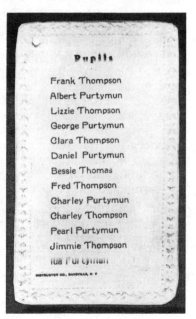

Pupils

Frank Thompson
Albert Purtymun
Lizzie Thompson
George Purtymun
Clara Thompson
Daniel Purtymun
Bessie Thomas
Fred Thompson
Charley Purtymun
Charley Thompson
Pearl Purtymun
Jimmie Thompson
Ida Purtymun

he finally tired out and tried to sneak off to take a nap, 13 year-old Pearl Purtymun found him and poured cold water in his face. He jumped up again as lively as ever.

One year later, Lizzie Thompson married Frank Nail in Flagstaff and bore him three daughters: Myrtle, Ivy and Maggie. Frank was killed in a railroad accident in 1911. Later, Lizzie married Jess Purtymun whose first wife had divorced him and left him with two children. Jess and Lizzie had five more children of their own. For several years Jess, Lizzie and their large family lived in a cave in Oak Creek Canyon until their home was built. For many years, Jess was a bootlegger particularly during Prohibition days. He had a number of stills throughout the canyon. Bootlegger Campground was named for Jess Purtymun.

With the marriage of Clara Thompson to Albert Purtymun, Margrett now had the company of her married daughter to enjoy. While Albert went off to earn a living in sawmills and lumber camps, Clara lived on and off with her mother and awaited the birth of her first child, Della Alberta, on May 30, 1904.

Despite a cabin full of family, Margrett Thompson was often isolated from other adults. When friends, family members or even strangers did visit, they were encouraged to stay for several days or weeks. Everyone visiting the canyon was always welcomed at the Thompson cabin, with one exception.

Often in the summer months, the mine executives from Jerome would leave their wives and children to enjoy a fishing vacation at Bacon Rind Park. Bacon Rind Park was located on Thompson property near Margrett's large garden.

One day while Margrett was picking green beans for supper, some 'painted ladies' wandered up to her and started visiting. The women were 'guests' of the mine executives from Jerome.

Innocently, Margrett returned the conversation while continuing to pick her beans. Her husband, J.J. came upon the scene and promptly yanked her home, scolding her for disgracing herself and warning her never to speak to those 'bad' women again. Her startled reply was, "but I was only picking beans."

When Margrett Thompson became a grandmother, she was still raising her own young sons: Charlie, age 11; Jimmie, nine, Albert, eight and Washington Green, age four.

After Clara's daughter, Della Alberta Purtymun (Della for short) turned seven, Margrett gave birth to her last child, Guy, in 1911. She was 47 years old at the time and J.J. was 69.

By then, Clara and Albert Purtymun had three more granddaughters for them to enjoy: Erma, Virginia and Laura. Between 1913 and 1925, these daughters would be joined by additional sisters and two brothers: Elsie, Violet, Zola, Albert and Charley. It was only natural, given these circumstances, that Clara's brothers - 'the boys' - would literally grow up with her own children.

Upper Oak Creek School, 1918 *This school began in 1918 and was used until 1943. It was located past the bridge at Slide Rock on the east side of the creek. (left to right) Agnes McGook (teacher), Laura Purtymun, Bertha Bennett, Vera Purtymun, Guy Thompson, Iva Nail, Maggie Nail, Della Purtymun, and Myrtle Nail. Photo courtesy of Laura Purtymun McBride*

The Second School in Oak Creek Canyon, 1904 *At first the school was held in a tent on the J.J. Thompson place until this cabin was built on the Charley Thompson property. (back row standing) an unidentified young man, Inez (Loy) Lay, Charley and Fred Thompson. (front row) Albert Thompson, Clara (Thompson) Purtymun who was visiting with her baby daughter, Della, Green Thompson and Jimmie Thompson. Photo courtesy of Laura Purtymun McBride*

Sedona's Family of Firsts, 1902 *(Back row standing) Frank Thompson (first white child born in Sedona), Jim M. James (son of the first family in Sedona). (sitting left to right) Albert W. Purtymun, Lizzie (Thompson) Purtymun, Clara (Thompson) Purtymun. Photo courtesy of Laura Purtymun McBride*

Two of Clara's daughters, Della and Laura, recounted the enriching experiences they had while being raised in Oak Creek Canyon near their beloved 'Grandma Thompson' and her boys.

If you have never tasted water dipped from the spring at Grandma Thompsons out of the big dipper, you have missed a lot, recalled Della. For as long as I can remember, that big dipper lay upside down in the fork of a tree next to the Spring House. The year I was born, (1904), my dad and uncle Frank built the Spring House out of red sand stones. They made shelves over the spring water, which ran inside, for grandma to keep her milk and butter cool. The Spring House had to be re-built again in 1916 by a stone mason because the sandstone had started to crumble from the water inside.

At Indian Gardens, all the buildings except the Spring House were built out of logs. There were two cabins, a smoke house, corn crib, chicken house and a barn. The barn had a door, but when it was filled with hay, it was kept shut. Whenever we fed the horses or cows, we had to climb up the logs to pitch the hay. The barn was also a good place to hide from 'the boys' when you had done something one of them didn't like. If you heard them coming up the logs on one side, you could go down the other side and run.

In 1910, the Thompson's log cabin was replaced by a house built with lumber. It had one big room with two regular size beds on one side and the fireplace and 'family room' on the other. A shed kitchen was built on the north side of this large room and a large open porch on the south side. The attic had an outside stairway to the boys' bedroom and the post office.

According to both Della and Laura, washing clothes and getting them white was quite a production for Grandma Thompson in the old days.

Grandma had a big black tub sitting on sandstones down by the spring. She built a fire under the tub after filling it with water. She rubbed the clothes on a washboard with some of the heated water, then they were tossed into the black tub where they were boiled while being stirred with a clothes-stick. A big bar of yellow laundry soap was shaved off in thin strips and added to the boiling water with some lye. That old laundry soap had a nice clean smell to it.

After the white clothes were boiled and stirred they were tossed into a tub of cold water, wrung out and put in a tub of rinse water which was as blue as the sky. This was made by tying two to three balls of bluing in a cloth and then dipping them into the rinse water.

Laura recalled a humorous incident that took place on one of

Grandma Thompson's washdays when Laura was about ten years old.

"Uncle Guy (who actually was a year younger than Laura) and I decided we wanted to smoke. So we got a corn cob out of the pig pen and hollowed it out. Then we took a dried vine to use as a stem for the pipe. Next, we had to decide what to smoke, so we stuffed the pipe with dried cow dung. Guy sent me into the house to get a match, but Grandma Thompson was in there and I knew she'd want to know what I needed a match for. So I told Guy we'd have to find another way to light the pipe. It was wash day, so Guy thought a hot coal from under Grandma Thompson's wash tub would do the trick. He'd just put the hot coal into the pipe and taken a puff when Grandma Thompson showed up. Guy stuffed the lit pipe into his back pocket to hide it. The coal burned his backside and Guy started jumping around and hollering "fire - fire," and leaped into Grandma's tub of rinse water. Of course I'm the one who got in trouble for smoking, not Grandma's youngest son, Uncle Guy.

Both Della and Laura were continually amazed at how Grandma Thompson managed to feed her huge family three times a day. Fresh hot biscuits were always a mainstay for each meal and most of the food they ate was raised there on the farm.

In the summer there were lots of fresh vegetables, plenty of fresh milk and homemade butter and a jar of Grandma's homemade preserves. The preserves were made from local peaches, Damson plums, green and ripe tomatoes and watermelon rinds.

Grandma made jelly from apple peelings, plums, wild grapes, elderberries and manzanita berries. In later years, Himalaya berries were introduced into the canyon by Grandma Purtymun Cook and today their blackberry-like fruit is still picked by locals and visitors throughout the canyon.

In the winter, Grandma Thompson kept a pot of beans simmering on the back of her wood-burning stove. Winter meals included plenty of potatoes, turnips, winter squash and cured meat from the smoke house. When Grandma made a cake, which she always mixed in a big lard pail, it was yellow as gold from all the fresh eggs she used. Usually she added black walnuts to her cake picked from the wild walnut trees growing near her home.

After each meal, Grandma Thompson took three biscuits to the back door to toss to the dogs, Shorty, Sport and Old Dash. That was all the food they were given, which made them good hunting dogs, particularly when it came to hunting for their own meals.

On the ridge east of the Thompson cabin, the red rocks formed a flat surface in two places. The children called the small flat the 'little playhouse' and the larger one the 'big play house.' Here all the cousins, brothers, young uncles and sisters would play. They

Sedona's First Homestead, 1880 *The first homestead in Sedona belonged to the Abraham James family. Today the area is known as Copper Cliffs and is located across Highway 179 from the Quality Inn. Photo courtesy of Laura Purtymun McBride*

lined the rooms of their play house with small rocks. The girls made their dolls out of everything from sticks, long shaped rocks, or an old, discarded summer squash in which they cut eyes and a mouth to make it look real.

'The boys' had a big can of marbles. After they made roads in the dirt, the marbles became horses, acorns became cows and small acorns were pigs.

The children played for hours with their homemade toys on their make-believe red rock playgrounds. During the winter months, they were not allowed to go to their playgrounds until the sun crept all the way down Wilson Mountain. The children would watch and wait. Then one of them would shout, 'sun's here,' and they all ran out to enjoy the remainder of the day.

"The worst thing children got in trouble for in the old days was stealing watermelons," recalled Laura. "I do remember helping my young uncles steal a chicken once. After we cleaned it, we tried to cook it on a stick over a campfire. It was so tough, we gave up on it."

After the Thompson and Purtymun children and grandchildren grew older, they would organize long hikes in the summer which usually included swimming in the creek, picnics and fishing. From March through August, summer time also was school time for all of the children living in the canyon.

Grandma Thompson's Spring House, 1989 *This is all that is left of the original J.J. Thompson homestead in Oak Creek Canyon. Photo by Kate Ruland-Thorne*

Love Message In Stone, *Albert Purtymun, who soon would marry Clara Thompson in 1901, etched their initials on the bottom of a pre-historic metate used by early area Indians to grind corn.*
This love message is now embedded in plaster on the side of their daughter Laura Purtymun McBride's home in Oak Creek Canyon. Photo by Kate Ruland-Thorne

But when Mattie and Steve Purtymun divorced and Mattie married Jim Cook, she and her children moved to Cook's ranch on the west side of Mingus Mountain near Jerome. After they left, school was held for awhile in a tent at Indian Gardens, then moved to Uncle Charley Thompson's home at Living Springs. Finally, everyone gave up on the idea of having a school in the canyon, so Grandma Thompson moved in the winter with her children and grandchildren to Red Rock so they could attend the school there. Clara or her mother, Grandma Thompson, lived in connecting tents on the Dumas Ranch (now Cresent Moon Ranch owned by the Forest Service) while school was in session.

The Red Rock School had been started by the Schuerman family in 1891. For many years, the teachers boarded with the Schuermans. Soon, more and more families wintered near the Red Rock School so their children could attend. As the student population grew, the school became the center of lively dances and numerous church services until it burned down in 1948.

It is interesting to note that all six Schuerman children were brought into the world with the help of one mid-wife, Elizabeth James, Grandma Thompson's mother. The history of the Schuerman and Dumas families, and others, will be included in Book Two.

Not long after his 75th birthday, Margrett's husband of 27 years, J.J. Thompson, died at his home in Indian Gardens in 1917. Margrett continued to live at her Indian Gardens home where most of her children and their families lived either with her or nearby.

Frank, Margrett and J.J.'s first born son, waited until late in life to marry. For years he hauled freight from Holbrook to Young and then became one of the first dry ranch farmers in Sedona. Frank's 160 acres of homesteaded land ran north from the present Oak Creek Marketplace in Uptown Sedona to Mormon Camp Wash, now the length of Jordan Road.

One day while Frank was looking through the NEEDLEWOMAN MAGAZINE, he found the name and address of Hilda Brown in England. Hilda had advertised in the magazine for a husband. So Frank wrote to her, and his 'Heart-and-Hand' bride arrived in Flagstaff with her daughter, Pearl. Frank identified her by the white carnation she was wearing. Hilda had disgraced herself by having Pearl out of wedlock. The couple had three children of their own, Jack, James and Margarett. Frank Thompson died in 1956 at the age of 74.

His mother, Grandma Thompson, continued to be loved and admired by all of her family "because she knew all the hardships of being a pioneer," said her granddaughter, Laura. "No matter how little she had, she always managed."

After Grandma Thompson moved to Indian Gardens, the only way to get in and out of the canyon until 1905 was by an old horse trail. There were all kinds of wild animals to worry about, including bears and mountain lions. Laura continued:

> Grandma never had more than four or five months of schooling, but she taught herself to read and write. When J.J. Thompson became the fourth territorial postmaster for Sedona in 1911, and started a post office at their home, Grandma Thompson was able to keep up with everything that was going on by reading the newspapers and magazines which arrived in the mail.
>
> Grandma started smoking cigarettes after Grandpa died. All of her boys smoked and when they weren't around, she'd take their Bull Durham tobacco, roll herself a cigarette and go for a walk in the woods. She didn't think anyone knew she was smoking, but all of us knew. We just didn't say anything about it because we knew how much it would embarrass her. 'Course Grandma James, her mother, always smoked a pipe and nobody thought anything about that."

Grandma (Margrett James) Thompson died in 1936 at the age of 72. Her daughter Clara remembered one of her mother's friends always saying that she often prayed for Mrs. Thompson. Clara was reminded of this after her mother's death and commented to her family that no one ever needed to pray for mother. "If anyone went to heaven, it had to be her."

Jessie J. (Bear) Howard ———┬——— Nancy Cline (1817-1910) (? -1861)		Elizabeth James (1828-1905)

Jess Howard
(1856 - 1923)

Martha (Mattie) Howard ———┬——— Stephen Purtymun James Cook
(1858 - 1951) (1855 - 1929)

(1) Emery Purtymun Maggie James
(1887-1947) (? -1938)

(2) Jess Purtymun ———┬——— Emma Arrowsmith Lizzie Thompson Nail
(1879-1956) (1884-1956)
Elmer Purtymun - Iva Nail
Lawerence Purtymun

(3) Albert W. Purtymun ———┬——— Clara Thompson
(1881-1961) (1887-1982)

Della Purtymun (1904-)	—	K. Greenwell (1904-)
Erma Purtymun (1906-1975)	—	W. Baker (1896-1951)
Virginia Purtymun (1908-)	—	B. Russell (1909-)
Laura Purtymun (1910-)	—	Ray McBride (1908-1979)
Elsie Purtymun (1913-1915)	—	
Violet Purtymun (1916-1977)	—	Bill Rupe
Albert Purtymun (1918-)	—	Minnie Hanson
Charley Purtymun (1921-1941)		
Zola Purtymun (1925-)	—	Peter Hernandez (1925-1973)

(4) George Purtymun Edith Sessions
(1884 - 1964)
(5) Charley Purtymun Mary Bostrom
(1888 - ?)
(6) Pearl Purtymun James Cook
(1891 - 1967)
(7) Ida Purtymun Robert Toube

GENEOLOGY Ragsdales, James and Howards

| Elizabeth Ragsdale (1828 - 1905) | Abraham James (1823 - 1881) | Bear Howard (1817 - 1910) |

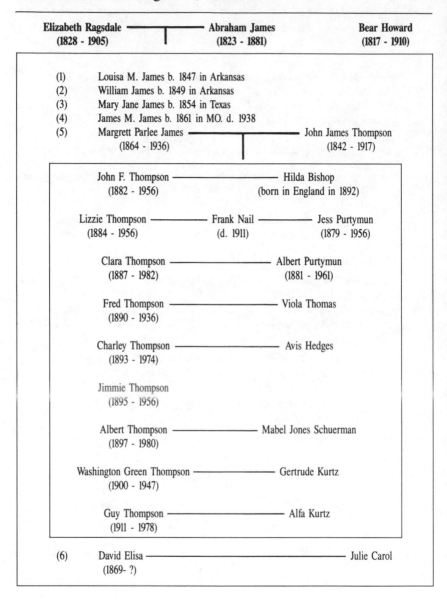

(1)   Louisa M. James b. 1847 in Arkansas
(2)   William James b. 1849 in Arkansas
(3)   Mary Jane James b. 1854 in Texas
(4)   James M. James b. 1861 in MO. d. 1938
(5)   Margrett Parlee James ———— John James Thompson
        (1864 - 1936)   (1842 - 1917)

    John F. Thompson ———————— Hilda Bishop
      (1882 - 1956)   (born in England in 1892)

    Lizzie Thompson ———— Frank Nail ———— Jess Purtymun
      (1884 - 1956)   (d. 1911)   (1879 - 1956)

      Clara Thompson ———————— Albert Purtymun
        (1887 - 1982)   (1881 - 1961)

      Fred Thompson ———————— Viola Thomas
        (1890 - 1936)

      Charley Thompson ———————— Avis Hedges
        (1893 - 1974)

      Jimmie Thompson
        (1895 - 1956)

      Albert Thompson ———————— Mabel Jones Schuerman
        (1897 - 1980)

    Washington Green Thompson ———————— Gertrude Kurtz
        (1900 - 1947)

      Guy Thompson ———————— Alfa Kurtz
        (1911 - 1978)

(6)   David Elisa ———————————————— Julie Carol
        (1869- ?)

Chapter Three
TALL TALES AND DOWNRIGHT LIES
The Story of Bear Howard

esse Jefferson Howard had reason to leave California. He was wanted for murder.

In the 1870's, Howard raised horses near Sacramento during the height of the range wars between cattlemen and sheepmen. Repeatedly Howard had warned the neighboring sheepman to keep his flocks off his land.

One day Howard rode out on his range and found a Mexican sheepherder sitting on a rock. Sheep were grazing all around. Howard ordered the Mexican off his property, but the Mexican only laughed and replied that his boss told him it was o.k. to graze there.

Enraged, Howard shot at the herder intending to scare him. Instead, the herder fell dead on the ground. To Howard's credit, he turned himself into the law and spent several days in jail. The sheriff, who was sympathetic toward Howard, left the jail door unlocked one night and Howard's daughter Mattie waited in the darkness with a horse. Howard was warned never to return to California again because the law would be looking for him.

When Howard arrived in Arizona Territory in 1880, he promptly changed his name to Charles Smith Howard and sought refuge in the rough-and-tumble wilderness of Oak Creek Canyon. There were no roads into the canyon then, only obscure Indian trails. It was a perfect place to hide out.

Eventually Howard earned the nickname of 'Bear' because of his prowess at killing bears in Oak Creek Canyon and selling the meat over the butcher's block in Flagstaff. Later, he returned to his earlier trade of raising horses.

Charles Smith 'Bear' Howard was the kind of character of which legends are made. He was over six feet tall and possessed all of the attributes of a mountain man of the Old West. He spent most of the remainder of his life in Oak Creek Canyon, and when he died 25 years after his arrival, there were more legends and downright lies told about him than any other character to settle in Northern Arizona.

But what would the Old West be like without its tall tales and larger-than-life characters? Most of the tales about Bear Howard are too fascinating to be ignored, and some do have elements of truth in them.

In a newspaper article called "ARIZONA DAYS," written February 9, 1969, by Rosco Wilson, the author claimed that the stories he was given about Bear Howard were offered on good authority by Morely and Fred Fox, members of a well-known cattle raising family in Pleasant Valley, Holbrook County. The following stories may be exaggerated, but they also attest to the fascination people had with the formidable Bear Howard, Sedona's most colorful character:

Bear Howard, had he lived in our day, would have been compared to a prehistoric man. He stood six foot eight in his stocking feet and did not reach his full strength until he passed age sixty. He obtained his nickname because he made a living killing bears at an age when most men would be thinking of retirement annuities. Although he was a quiet and peaceful man, he could not tolerate being teased or tormented.

When Howard first arrived in Northern Arizona, there was no railroad yet and the Pony Express still carried the mail. The principle business in the Flagstaff area then was raising long-horned cattle and lumber.

The biggest outfit of all was the Hashknife Cattle Company. From wrangler to cook, the Hashknife men were the roughest, toughest, fightingest bunch of punchers ever assembled on any old-time cattle spreads in the Southwest. Many of them had been forced to leave states further east. They were a hard-driving crew who feared neither man nor beast.

Now when the Hashknife boys rode into a town, one of their most popular sports was badgering the townspeople, who usually were too terrified to fight back. On one of these occasions, a group of the Hashknife boys ran into Bear Howard in a Flagstaff saloon. Howard looked like a big innocent yokel so Corney Wallace, leader of this local gang, motioned Howard to the center of the floor and commanded him to dance to the rag-time syncopation of his six guns. Bear never cracked a smile. He obeyed orders and was soon giving a fair imitation of a heavy Irish clog dance to the vast amusement of Wallace and his friends.

Wallace made the mistake of not keeping out of range of Bear Howard's size 16 feet. As deliberately as a cat stalks a mouse, Howard's right foot suddenly arched from the floor with a violent swish and a sickening thud catching Wallace under the chin. The cowboy's heavy frame spun upward and his six guns clattered to the floor. Bear pounced on his prone antagonist with an agility that belied his bulk. Fists as hard as Malapai boulders tore into Wallace's face, peeling the skin back to his ears. Stunned at the sudden turn of events, the cowboy's friends never made a move to save him from this terrible thrashing.

After kicking Wallace into a corner, Bear fastened his malignant gaze on the other cowboys and taunted, "if there is any other s.o.b. who wants to watch me dance, step forward and he'll find me mighty accommodating."

For a few seconds, nobody dared to move. Then as one, the crowd left by the nearest door. They were used to drunken brawls and feats of strength, but this man's power was superhuman.

Bear quietly finished his drinking and it wasn't until he left for his cabin in Oak Creek Canyon that Wallace's friends returned to pack him to the town druggist-doctor who sewed 29 stitches in his ripped up face. It is also worth noting that Bear Howard had celebrated his 67th birthday only a few days before.

In the same article, the author described Bear Howard's past and offered a Paul Bunyan-like description of his appearance:

Picture if you can, this giant of a man whose muscles and sinew bulged all over his huge frame. His hands were like twin hammers of poured steel. Each shoe required the hide of a yearling beef His hair, which he never bothered to comb, added to the impression of his wild power. The Almighty gave him teeth unlike those of other men. He walked with a military air and his stride when hitting the trail was long and graceful. His speech was slow and pleasant, except when he was angered, and then it rumbled up from the caverns of his chest with all the fury of an active volcano.

Howard sported a bullet which was still lodged in his back. It was fired at him by one of Santa Anna's soldiers in the Mexican War. He always liked to tell what the Mexican got in return.

"When the ball hit me," he said, "I played like I was hurt bad and rolled down into a little wash knowin' this chili-eater would be comin' over to see what he could snitch off my carcass I had my bayonet ready and when he looked over the top of the wash, all unsuspectin-like, I give it to him right between the eyes. That sure was a surprised Mexican. I had to put my boots across his mouth 'fore I could work that knife loose. Naw, I weren't hurt bad."

With the war's end, Howard was mustered out of the Army and went to California where the gold rush was on. He made a rich stake but was swindled out of it by his blackguard brother. Later he homesteaded a farm and prospered until he had trouble with sheepherders. His corn and barley fields were a temptation to every herder in that part of the state and they turned their sheep in his fields whenever they thought he wasn't looking. One day in a fit of temper, he shot a dozen sheep and two or three herders. The sheriff was sent to arrest him. He fled to the hills but was caught. A jury convicted him and he was sentenced to jail. He sawed his way out and came to Arizona to relax and grow old.

According to Howard's family records, Jesse Jefferson Howard was born in Illinois in 1817 and was of Scotch-Irish descent. When he was 19, he enlisted to fight in the war between Texas and Mexico and served under Sam Houston. He was shot in the back and carried a bullet in his lung for 54 years. When he was well into his sixties, a doctor in Flagstaff finally cut it out. It was such a long heavy bullet, that the doctor asked to keep it as pay for the surgery.

When Bear entered the doctor's office to have the surgery, he noticed two big men there and asked what they were doing. The doctor had hired them to hold Bear down while he cut out the bullet, since there was no anesthetic. Bear waved the men away, saying that wouldn't be necessary.

After Howard mustered out of the army in the 1840's, he headed for the gold fields of California in 1849. He settled near Ventura in a town named Hornitos (now under water). There Howard met and married a little Dutch girl named Nancy Cline who bore him two children. One, Jess, was born in 1856 and a daughter, Martha (Mattie), in 1858. When Mattie was three years old, their mother died. Howard moved his children to Santa Clara and enrolled them in a Spanish Mission. He started another horse ranch nearby.

By the time Mattie was six and her brother was eight, their father was teaching them to ride bareback and shoot a gun. Mattie thought nothing of grabbing a horse by the mane and pulling herself up, galloping full speed with her long raven hair flying in the wind.

On one occasion when she was a young girl out riding, she saw two men coming up the road. These were dangerous times, and her father had warned her never to speak to strangers. Mattie didn't realize the men were surveyors, so she spurred her horse and fled. When the men got into town, they told everyone about seeing an Indian princess riding bareback with her black hair streaming behind her. Apparently they found out later that it was Mattie Howard because they named a mountain near Ventura 'Mount Mattie' in her honor.

On another occasion, when the two Howard children were small, their father left them in the care of an old Chinaman while he went to town. Indians rode up and kidnaped the children, escaping down an old Indian trail. Howard, returning home by way of the same

Bear Howard's Cabin, 1890. This was built at the mouth of West Fork. Later his improvements were sold to John Thomas, Sr. (seated with a rifle). Eventually the cabin was replaced by Mayhew's Oak Creek Lodge. Photo courtesy of Laura Purtymun McBride

The Howard-Purtymun Family, 1891. (back row - left to right) Emery Purtymun, Jess Howard, Bear Howard. (second row) Jess Purtymun, Martha (Mattie Purtymun with baby Pearl, Stephen Purtymun with Charley, Albert Purtymun, George Purtymun, Dan Purtymun seated on floor. Photo courtesy of Laura Purtymun McBride

Sedona's Legendary Character, 1890. The man towering in the middle is Bear Howard with his rifle, hunting dogs and the two bears he killed. Photo courtesy of Laura Purtymun McBride

The Cave House, 1918. Bear Howard's grandson, Jess Purtymun, plays an accordion outside his 'cave house' in Oak Creek Canyon. The writing on the rock to the right says, 'Our cave kitchen - 1918 - Oak Creek. Photo courtesy of Laura Purtymun McBride

Bear Howard, 1905

trail with several other men, ran into these Indians who promptly tossed both children into a cactus patch. Howard and his friends took out after them.

The old Chinaman found the children and hid them in a mine shaft through the night while Howard pursued the Indians and fought it out with them.

Some time after Jess and Mattie Howard were grown, their father was forced to leave California because of the incident with the sheepherder. Howard's brothers continued to raise horses in California and one of their horses eventually sired the great race horse, Man-O-War.

When Howard left California for Arizona Territory in the late 1870's, his daughter Mattie was already married to Stephen Purtymun and had one small son Emery. Their second son Jess (named for her brother) was born in Ventura, California in 1879. Shortly after Jess's birth the Purtymans set out for Arizona in order to be near Bear Howard. Mattie's brother Jesse traveled with them.

Not long after the Purtymans and Jesse Howard arrived in southern Arizona, they came across the horrible massacre of a wagon train. They sought the soldiers at a nearby fort to escort them as far as Prescott. After they visited Bear Howard in Oak Creek Canyon, the Purtymans moved to Old Pinal (near Phoenix) where Stephen worked as a freighter.

In old Pinal, their third and fourth sons, Albert and George, were born in 1881 and 1884. Their next son Dan was born in Mesa in 1886. By then, the Purtymans' were ready to move back to Oak Creek Canyon. They lived for a while in a tent near Bear Howard's cabin at the mouth of West Fork. Later, the Purtymans moved to the old Pump House area eight miles south of Flagstaff where they lived in a log cabin. Mattie told her grandchildren in later years about the chilling experience of listening to (mountain) lions scream each night.

Stephen Purtymun continued to haul freight, work in mines and farm. In 1896, he moved his family to a flat across the creek from the present Junipine Resort. By now his family consisted of nine children, six boys and three girls. Their second daughter, Ruby, died in infancy. Number six son Charley was born in 1888 followed by daughters Pearl (1891) and Ida (1892).

On their new land, Stephen built a large, beautiful log cabin with a bay window and planted fruit trees. Nearly 100 years later, the cabin remains intact and well preserved with many of the Purtymun's original fruit trees still bearing fruit.

In 1891, when Pearl Purtymun was born, her grandfather, Bear Howard, took another wife. She was Elizabeth James, widow of Abraham James, Sedona's first settler. Howard was 64 years old by then and Elizabeth was 54. The marriage lasted three months.

Depending on which side of the family tells the story, the two reasons given for the breakup of the marriage were: Elizabeth didn't like sleeping with Bear Howard's three big dogs, and Elizabeth didn't like Howard's generosity, particularly with her cattle. He had a tendency to give them away if someone said they needed them. Probably both stories are true, and there is little question that the breakup was entirely Elizabeth's idea. This would not be the only divorce in the family.

Six years later, Mattie divorced Stephen, her husband of 22 years, because 'he drank too much.' Her youngest daughter, Ida, was only five years old when the family broke up. Shortly afterwards Mattie married James Cook. She helped raise Cook's five children on Cook's horse and cattle ranch near Jerome's Mingus Mountain. Every year, Cook rode the freight train with his horses to the market back east. He always returned with presents for everyone. Unfortunately there was another side to Jim Cook according to family members. He too was inclined to drink too much, and was a notorious womanizer. Mattie finally divorced him as well.

Mattie Howard Purtymun Cook would be remembered as an expert seamstress. She made hundreds of quilts and was known for her fine knitting and crocheting. Mattie outlived her two husbands and four of her children. She died in 1951, just a few months short of her 94th birthday.

Mattie's first husband, Stephen, moved back to California after their divorce and started a small country store in Northfork, California. He also married a second time. His children and friends called him Father and referred to his second wife as 'Father's wife.' Whenever his children visited him in California, he entertained them on the second floor of his home, and his new wife always entertained her children from another marriage on the first floor.

When Stephen had a stroke, his daughter Pearl took care of him until his death in 1929. She was the only one of his children who attended his funeral.

Jess Howard, Bear Howard's son, never married. He worked the mines around Superior and later homesteaded on Oak Creek where the Garland's Lodge now stands. The kitchen at the lodge was built around Jess Howard's original log cabin. Jess Howard died in 1923 at the home of his nephew, Albert who was married to Clara Thompson Purtymun.

Old Bear Howard lived to the age of 93. Clara Thompson Purtymun remembered him as an outstanding man. Grandpa Howard, as he was called, stayed with her one time when she was pregnant. The family lived in a tent near Dewey at the time, and all of their water had to be hauled from the creek. Clara said that as old as he was, Grandpa Howard wouldn't let her do anything and waited on her hand and foot. She thought perhaps it was because he had lost his first wife when she was very young.

When Bear Howard first settled in Oak Creek Canyon, he only took Squatter's Rights on his property in West Fork. After Bear Howard's death in 1910, Mattie sold her father's improvements to

The Cave House, *1989. Laura Purtymun McBride studies her uncle Jess Purtymun's cave house as it appears today.*

The Purtymun Home, *1989. Laura Purtymun McBride stands outside the well-preserved Purtymun home near Junipine Resort in Oak Creek Canyon. The home was built in 1897.*

Photos by Kate Ruland-Thorne

V.L. Thomas, a local range rider. Thomas and his three sons proved up on the property which, extended from West Fork to the present Don Hoel's Cabins in Oak Creek Canyon.

By 1925, Bear Howard's original property had been purchased by the Mayhews, who built the famous Oak Creek Lodge there. Mayhew's Oak Creek Lodge became the favorite stopping place for movie stars and dignitaries. All who stayed there heard the legends of Bear Howard. They heard other legends as well, like the story of the lost Spanish treasure in Sycamore canyon. That mine was touted as being so rich that the Spanish had to melt down the gold and make it into bars before they could wheel it out of the canyon on old wooden carts.

One day, a guest at the Mayhew's Lodge went hiking over the mountain and ended up in Sycamore Canyon. When he returned, he claimed he found the Spanish mine with all the gold bars still intact. He also said he found a leather-bound book, written in Spanish. It had Bear Howard's name on it. The man claimed he went back many times, but never again found the mine. No one was ever shown the leather-bound book either. But the man's story was taken as truth, and people have been looking for the 'lost Spanish mine' ever since.

The Mayhews' famous lodge burned to the ground in the 1980's. Its remains can still be seen near the trail head at West Fork. Although the lodge is gone, the stories of West Fork's first settler, Bear Howard, live on. The last legend about Bear Howard was that, when he died in 1910, his body was found with a bear cub in his lap. That story has been pronounced as a downright lie...or is it a tall tale?

Chapter Four
THE LIFE AND TIMES OF
CARL AND SEDONA SCHNEBLY

s far as Sedona Miller Schnebly's father was concerned, she had no business running off to Indian Territory with that infernal husband of hers, Carl. As a last resort, Philip Miller issued a warning. "If you go," he said, "I'll write you out of my will." Sedona went, and Philip Miller made good his threat.

How wrenching it must have been to defy her father and move away from her family and friends in Gorin, Missouri, the town of her birth. How terrified she must have felt arriving with her two small children in the wild and raucous mining town of Jerome. There Carl, who had gone ahead two weeks before, met them at the train and took them by wagon over a rough road into an uncivilized unknown.

What were Sedona Schnebly's thoughts and feelings when Carl showed her the land he had bought along the banks of Oak Creek? Did she thrill to the jagged walls of red rock that surrounded her, or did they overpower her and fill her with fear? There was no home to live in when she arrived. That would have to be built later. She must make do with an old run down bunkhouse and later a tent.

But Carl Schnebly was filled with plans and dreams, and they were infectious. Together they would show Philip Miller how wrong he had been. Besides, Sedona loved Carl Schnebly with all of her being. She had married him over her father's objections, and now she had no choice but to follow him wherever he went. His dreams became her dreams. Together they would make something of this land, something they would be proud of. And in time, with prayers, hard work and lots of luck, they would succeed.

The year was 1901 when the Schneblys arrived at their new home. There were untold adjustments for Sedona to make. Always before, she had sisters to share her feelings with and a mother to turn to when she needed advice. Now there was only Carl and her two babies, Elsworth and Pearl. The loneliness must have been terrible, quite like the loneliness experienced by so many other pioneer wives who wrote often of it in their diaries and letters.

Then too, there was so much work to be done and without any conveniences to lighten the load. There was no store nearby, no post office. Neighbors lived far away, and doctors were almost non-existent. But Sedona Schnebly was made of strong stuff. Although she had been raised in a wealthy home by prominent parents, she knew how to work, she knew how to cook and she knew how to make the best of things.

Sedona Arabella Miller was the sixth child and second daughter born to a Pennsylvania Dutch couple, Philip and Amanda Miller. The Millers had five more daughters and another son after Sedona was born, but none of their other eleven children was given a more unusual name. When asked years later why she gave her daughter this name, Amanda Miller explained that she had never heard the name before, she simply made it up. "After all, there is a first time for any name or word," she said.

Sedona's father, Philip Miller, was the second largest landowner in the Gorin area. His farm stretched toward the nearby town of Edna. When Sedona was born, Gorin was not yet a town. In fact it was called Octavia then and was merely a collection of farms made up of pasture, timberland and rough horse trails. Mail was deposited in leather pouches tacked up and down an old elm tree. It was from around this elm tree that the town of Gorin eventually sprouted.

About one mile east of this elm tree, a little log cabin served as a schoolhouse. For awhile it also served as a church on Sundays for the three predominant religions of the area: Methodist, Baptist and Presbyterian. The Millers were staunch Methodists, a matter that would affect Sedona's life twenty years later when she met, and then defied her father by marrying, Theodore Carleton (T.C.) Schnebly. Carl Schnebly was an equally staunch 'predestination' Presbyterian.

When Sedona was ten years old, the Atchison, Topeka, and Santa Fe Railroad Company began construction of a division of their road from Kansas City to Chicago. Gorin, located in the northern corner of Missouri, lay right in the path the railroad planned to cross. When the railroad executives arrived to obtain land right-of-ways on which to lay their track, they liberally paid one Philip Miller for the use of much of the land they needed.

By 1887, the first train finally passed through Gorin, and hundreds of people flocked to the tracks to see the sight. Most had never seen a train before. Unquestionably, the Miller family was in full attendance.

After the railroad came, a building boom followed and Gorin, Missouri, was officially incorporated as a town in 1887. The post office was moved inside a building and Philip Miller eventually served as Gorin's fourth postmaster.

Along the railroad tracks, a grist mill and a flour mill sprang up, and near the depot a pickle factory opened. The farmers who

Sedona Miller, *1890's*

Photo courtesy of Paula Schnebly Hokanson

raised wheat and cucumbers prospered. Philip Miller was one of them.

But despite all the prosperity that the town, or Philip Miller and his family enjoyed, the Miller children were expected to live by the Protestant work ethic and work in the fields on the family farm. The Miller children did not live a pampered life but one that was structured, genteel and imbued with solid Methodist teachings.

Sedona was rarely called by her given name. Throughout her life, family and friends called her "Dona." When she was small, some even referred to her as "that little pop-eyed Donie Miller."

Although Dona's life was a simple one, Philip Miller did believe in educating his children. Dona and her siblings were sent to a private finishing school, the Gorin Academy. All spoke German as fluently as they did English, and we know Sedona had elocution, piano and organ lessons.

After finishing her own education, Sedona taught school for awhile. Then at some point before her 20th birthday, she met her future husband, Carl.

Theodore Carleton Schnebly was born near Hagerstown, Maryland, on December 29, 1868. He was the fourth of twelve children born to Daniel Henry, Jr., and Maria Elizabeth Davis Schnebly. Carl's family moved to Kahoka, Missouri, when he was still a small boy. Carl's close-knit family were devout Presbyterians. All worked hard on their family farm, too. When Carl and his four brothers graduated from high school, each earned degrees at Kahoka College. Like Philip and Amanda Miller, the Schnebly family descended from Pennsylvania Dutch stock.

The term 'Pennsylvania Dutch' was coined by early English colonists who really meant to say 'Deutsh,' meaning German. The term soon became corrupted to mean Dutch. It was a name applied to those Germans and Swiss who migrated by the thousands to America in the 1700's and who settled primarily in south-central and eastern Pennsylvania and in Maryland.

Carl's great-grandfather, Dr. Heinrich Schnebly, emigrated from Zurich, Switzerland, to America in 1750 at the age of 22. Shortly after he arrived in America, he became very ill. When he finally recovered, all of his savings were gone and he had to walk from New York to Washington County, Maryland, where many of his Swiss companions had settled. Through skill, industry and the practice of medicine, "Dr. Henry" eventually acquired an enormous tract of land called the "Garden of Eden," five miles north of Hagerstown, Maryland, where Carl was born. When Dr. Henry died at the age of 77, he was one of the largest landholders in Washington County. He also owned vast tracts of land in Kentucky and West Virginia.

Dr. Henry and his first wife Elizabeth Snavely had four sons, Henry, John, Jacob and David and a daughter, Elizabeth. He had no children by his second wife Catherine Wetsol. Dr. Henry left a farm to each grandchild who was named after him, hence a family genealogy rife with the name Henry. Theodore Carleton's father, Daniel Henry, Jr., very likely was one of Dr. Henry's fortunate grandchildren.

By 1894, Carl Schnebly and three of his four brothers, William, Jacob, and Elsworth, had formed a partnership in a hardware store in Gorin, Missouri. It was about this time that Carl began to court Sedona Miller. Despite the fact that Carl and Sedona shared the same Pennsylvania Dutch roots, that Carl descended from a prominent family, and that he was an established businessman with a college education, Philip Miller neither liked nor approved of Carl's courtship with his daughter and tried to dissuade her from seeing him.

"Why," he must have nagged Sedona, "don't you find a nice young man like Loring Johnson?"

Loring Johnson was a charming, handsome man who owned a clothing business. While Carl was courting Sedona, Loring was courting Sedona's sister, Lillie Victoria. Both young couples planned their weddings in the same year. The big plus for Loring, as far as Philip Miller was concerned was that Loring was a Methodist. A common wag among the town gossips at that time was that Philip Miller was getting 100 sons-in-law. "Loring was one and Carl was double zeros."

Over her father's objections, Sedona Arabella married Carl

Schnebly on her 20th birthday, February 24, 1897, and six months later, Lillie Victoria married Loring Johnson. Years later, to the horror of the family, and the town of Gorin, Loring Johnson was convicted of embezzlement and served time in both Leavenworth and San Quentin Prisons.

When each of Philip Miller's children married, he built them a new home as a wedding gift. There is some indication that this was not offered to Sedona and Carl, or perhaps Carl refused the offer. One thing is certain, Carl was giving serious consideration to moving his family away from Gorin and into 'Indian country.' It was a decision which caused the final break with Philip, who threatened to write Sedona out of his will if she and Carl went through with their plans.

But Carl's brother Elsworth whose health was poor, had already gone to Arizona Territory in 1898 in the hope that a better climate might bring about better health. Elsworth found his way into the red rock country of north central Arizona, bought a burro, a bed roll and a camp outfit and for the next few years, hunted and fished up and down Oak Creek Canyon. As Elsworth's health improved, he regularly wrote to his brothers extolling the virtues of this magnificent country and urging them to join him.

In the fall of 1901, Carl decided to act upon his brother's suggestion, and Philip Miller made good his threat to write his daughter out of his will.

On October 12, 1901, Carl Schnebly arrived in Jerome Junction, Arizona Territory via Flagstaff on a Santa Fe "emigrant" train. One car of the train was loaded with all the family possessions including furniture, farm equipment and a team of horses. Carl had no choice but to leave everything but his horses on the side of the mountain for awhile until he could retrieve them. Carl was assured by a member of the Farley family (who later became Sedona residents) that everything would remain safe. Eleven days later, Sedona and the Schneblys' two children, Elsworth, age three and Pearl, age two, also arrived in Jerome. Carl took them by wagon over a rough, rocky, sandy wagon track to their new home.

The family arrived in a place known by some as Upper Oak Creek Crossing and by others as Camp Garden. Those others consisted of about five families. Old J.J. Thompson's family still lived at Indian Gardens. Among the other families were the Armijo and Chavez families and the Schuerman and Dumas families. Most had arrived in the area in the late 1880's.

When Carl finally was able to return to Jerome to retrieve the family goods, he found them intact and undisturbed. He had settled his family on an 80-acre farm which his brother Elsworth had purchased from the Frank Owenby family. On this same land eight decades later, the city of Sedona's famous Los Abrigados Resort would be built.

When the Schneblys first settled on their new land, there was

Philip and
Amanda Miller,
1890's

Sedona and
Carl Schnebly,
1897

Trip Down the Grand Canyon
*1903. Sedona is on third mule
with Carl behind her holding
Genivieve.*

Elsworth, born May 11,
1898, *with his mother.*

Photos courtesy of Paula Schnebly Hokanson

only a bunkhouse on the place for them to live in. Carl planned a large home, but it would take many months of travel back and forth to Flagstaff to collect enough lumber for the project.

In those days, the only way to get to Flagstaff was by following the old Beaver Head stagecoach road. The stage site, located today 11 miles south of Sedona off Hwy. 179, was built in 1876 and abandoned in 1882. In its heyday, the stage carried passengers through the struggling young territory from Prescott to Santa Fe, N.M.

Until 1902, the stage line trail was the only wagon road north out of the Verde Valley. For a loaded wagon, the 60-mile journey took almost a week to travel. After the stage line was abandoned in 1882, the route became known as the Verde Valley Wagon Road.

But Carl soon discovered there were shorter routes to Flagstaff. One in particular went straight up a mountain. It was primarily a cattle trail created by a Flagstaff rancher named Munds. Going straight up over the mountain reduced travel time one-way to only two days.

J.J. Thompson had contracted with Coconino County to complete the road, which had been worked on for several years by other pioneer families. It didn't take long for Carl's shrewd business mind to figure out that reducing travel time by several days would allow him to get fresh produce quickly to the lucrative Flagstaff market. According to Coconino County records, Carl and his brother Elsworth were both paid to help the road crew transform the last ten miles of the trail into a usable wagon road which we know today as Schnebly Hill Road.

The Coconino County supervisors approved the road in 1902. Several families in the Verde Valley contributed $300 and Carl added $300 of his own.

The construction crew used only picks and shovels. Whenever the road had to be dynamited, the holes for the dynamite were hand-drilled into the rocks. All the men worked 12 hours a day for $1 a day and stayed on the job for over six months until the road was completed.

In the late summer of 1902, Carl already was trucking produce up the Schnebly Hill Road to Flagstaff. When market-bound, Carl would leave his creek-side home in the late evening and drive to the last level spot between his home and the top of the mountain. There he camped out for the night. After feeding and watering his four horses, he turned two of them loose to go home. By early morning, Carl continued the long, all day journey to Flagstaff. He returned home within three days with lumber for his new home and, later, supplies for his small store. He often brought visitors back to Sedona who camped out in tents on the Schnebly property.

Once completed, the Schneblys' new home was a two-story, eleven-room frame house with a basement that measured 30 x 32 feet. The old bunkhouse was turned over to young Pearl and

The Schnebly home, *1902-1907.*

"Tad" (Elsworth) with his
sister Pearl, *1900.*

The Schnebly Family in Sedona
prior to Pearl's death, *1905.*

Photos courtesy of Paula Schnebly Hokanson

Elsworth for a playhouse. Elsworth remembered that he and Pearl would pick their father's luscious strawberries and use them to decorate their mud pies after 'baking' them in the old bunkhouse stove.

Before long, the Schnebly home was known as a place where one could stay the night and enjoy a good meal. The Schnebly home was not referred to as a hotel until many years later. A hotel was never the building's original purpose.

The journey between Flagstaff and Jerome was such a long and arduous one that people just naturally wanted to stop over along the way, and the Schneblys owned the only home large enough to accommodate paying guests. In time, the Schneblys also rented tents on their property as more and more people chose to remain. Sedona's reputation as an excellent cook added to people's desire to linger. Guests came often to hunt and fish while others stayed for months seeking to improve their health in the pristine climate. Board and room never exceeded a dollar a day.

One such guest was a reporter, Harry Quimby, of a Boston newspaper, the Union Manchester. In 1903, Quimby filled three full pages of his paper with descriptions of the paradise he had discovered in Arizona and the charming family he stayed with for three weeks, a Mr. Carl Schnebly and his lovely wife, Sedona. Here is an excerpt from his story.

> Mr. Schnebly puts most of his efforts in his garden and markets his products in Flagstaff making two trips a week in the busy season. His loads average him $60 a trip and many of them amount to over $100 during the busy season. The prices he gets for his fresh produce would make many a New England housewife resort to the canned variety. He markets nothing less than $5 per hundred: Sweet corn brings 35c a dozen, tomatoes, 8 1/3c a pound, watermelons 5c a pound, and cantaloupe, cauliflower and summer squash, 8 1/3c a pound. Berries in very small boxes fetch him 20c a pound while he gets as high as 8 1/3c a pound for his apples and peaches. Some of these prices are wholesale at that.
>
> Mr. Schnebly also runs a small store here where a visitor can buy bacon, flour or tobacco. By this means, he always has a load both ways on his trips to Flagstaff.
>
> His wife, Sedona, operates a small summer hotel and it is an ideal place to rest and study some of Arizona's finest scenery. Of course Oak Creek Canyon is not to be compared with the Grand Canyon for grandeur, but it surely reminds one of that place.
>
> Mr. Schnebly's ranch is also a post office having mail twice a week. It is carried over a star route of 20 miles. I was here on election day and it was surely a quiet election. There were hardly enough permanent voters to fill the offices. There were twelve votes cast, all Democratic.

After only two years from the time of their arrival in the area, it can be said that Carl and Sedona's drive and industry were primarily responsible for turning their little hamlet into something that had the makings of a town. Not only had the Schneblys established the area's first hotel, grocery store, profitable truck farm (and if one wants to stretch it - health spa), Carl housed the first post office and served as the area's first postmaster.

Initially when Carl applied for the first post office, he submitted the names of Oak Creek Crossing and Schnebly Station to the Postmaster General in Washington, D.C. Both names were rejected because the cancellation stamp couldn't handle that many words. It was Elsworth, Carl's brother, who suggested he call the new town Sedona. "Why don't we name it after Dona?" he asked one day during breakfast. Carl seized upon the idea. So at the young age of 25, Sedona Arabella's unusual name was established for posterity, and she became known as the mother of the town. Today, residents can be grateful that Sedona's mother did not give her a more ordinary name like Mildred.

When Goldie Genevieve was born on October 22, 1903, Sedona really had her hands full. With Carl gone most of the time hauling produce back and forth to Flagstaff, the majority of the chores around their ranch were left to her.

Not only did she cook and clean for her family, but for their numerous guests as well. Laundry had to be washed in tubs by the creek. Wearing Carl's overalls, Sedona worked in the garden and helped herd and brand their cattle. Like most pioneer women, Sedona sewed all the family clothes, made her own soap, canned tons of fruits and vegetables and became adept at killing rattlesnakes with a broom handle.

Somehow, she found time to gather her guests and area residents together for an occasional sing-a-long or a non-denominational church service in her home on Sundays. Sometimes a visiting preacher showed up to give a sermon, but most of the time the services consisted of Bible reading and hymn singing with Sedona providing the accompaniment on her prized piano.

By 1904, the Schneblys did hire a Chinese cook. Young Elsworth recalled that the old man did not like cats. Whenever one of the family cats invaded his kitchen, he would threaten to "putee it into the lice soup."

Holidays were particularly special in the Schnebly home. Invitations to their Thanksgiving feasts were prized, so much so that 50 years later, Dr. Ralph Palmer remembered his Thanksgiving dinner with the Schneblys in his book, DOCTOR ON HORSEBACK:

> On Thanksgiving, we rode to the Schnebly ranch. The Schneblys were sure good providers in the food line. There were some twenty of us at a long table with a haunch of

venison at one end and a roasted whole pig at the other. On one side was a turkey and the other a goose, both stuffed and roasted. One of the vegetables which particularly impressed me was a large squash stuffed with cabbage and baked.

Despite the incredible work load and tremendous responsibilities, Sedona and Carl were happier than they had ever been. Their lives were filled with love, good friends and productivity. Unfortunately, fate intervened, and one day a dreadful tragedy would put an end to their dreams and to their growing prosperity.

On June 12, 1905, Sedona, her son Elsworth, then age seven, and Pearl, age five, were herding milk cows. Sedona held baby Genevieve in the saddle in front of her as she rode. As young as they were, Elsworth and Pearl were already skilled at riding their well-trained, gentle cow ponies.

It was always a pleasant chore to bring in the milk cows each evening, particularly in the early summer when the air was cool and the light from the setting sun gave the red rocks a shimmering, fiery glow. It was one chore Sedona and the children looked forward to. Often on these occasions, she and the children searched for arrowheads or christened rock formations with new and funny names.

But on that particular day, five year-old Pearl, her sun bonnet tied securely around her neck, started down a steep embankment. One story is that she wanted to retrieve an arrow head she had spotted. Childlike, she looped the reins around her neck in order to have her hands free to reach her prize. Seeing this, her mother shouted a warning, but it was too late. A cow suddenly broke from the herd and Pearl's well-trained pony started after it. Pearl wildly clutched at her saddle as the pony pivoted. She was thrown over the pony's neck only to be jerked, trampled and dragged to death as the terrified pony dashed madly toward home.

Elsworth recalled that tragic day many years later and added that it was a sight never to be erased from his memory:

It was a wild and terrifying ride down the banks toward home. Mother frantically urged her horse to go faster while holding on to Genevieve for dear life. Some men working nearby saw Pearl's pony racing home and knew something was wrong. They arrived ahead of Mother and carried the battered body of little Pearl into the house. I picked up one of Pearl's shoes in the doorway.

All that was left of Pearl's clothing was the bonnet strings still tied securely around her neck. The accident was horrible beyond belief for Sedona, who blamed herself. She cut up her lovely wedding dress to make Pearl's shroud. Grandma Thompson, J.J. 's wife, came down from the canyon to help prepare the little girl for burial.

Pearl was buried in the Schnebly's front yard, and every time Sedona looked out her window, she was reminded of that dreadful day. Before long, she began to withdraw into a world of her own, and her once robust health rapidly faded. As Sedona's health continued to decline, the doctors told Carl to move his wife away before her haunting memory took an irreversible toll. Four months later, the Schneblys returned to Gorin, Missouri.

After arriving in Gorin, Carl took a job with the Prairie Oil and Gas Company as a lineman and Sedona made peace with her father, who died of complications during surgery nine months later.

Sedona's youngest sister Pearl, age 18, recently had died also, so the Millers and Schneblys had grief to share. This very likely helped soften Philip Miller's once hardened heart.

After Philip Miller died, the Schneblys left Gorin for Memphis, Missouri, where Carl went into the clothing business with his brother-in-law Loring Johnson. A year later, the Schnebly's second son, Daniel Henry, named for Carl's father, was born on August 22, 1907. The birth of a new baby helped to heal Sedona's broken heart.

Although the partnership with his scheming brother-in-law, Loring, lasted four years, one can only speculate as to whether Carl fell victim to Loring's fraudulent practices. What is apparent is that the Schneblys left Missouri with very little capital to invest when Carl decided to return to farming.

The Schneblys did not return to Arizona because Carl's older brother Elsworth, who could not keep up the prodigious work load on the Schnebly ranch, already had sold it and gone back into teaching. Several years later, the eleven-room ranch house, then owned by the Black family, burned to the ground. The Blacks are the ones who referred to the original Schnebly home as a hotel.

Carl's only chance to own land again was to homestead it, so he moved his family to Boyero, Colorado, where homestead land was still available and where some of their Missouri friends had settled. Carl filed for his first homestead on September 22, 1910. In Boyero, the last of their six children were born: Clara Amanda on January 31, 1912, and Margaret Elizabeth on June 30, 1915. Sedona was 38 years old when Margaret was born.

Clara still has vivid recollections of the Schneblys' life in Boyero, a town of about 100 citizens. Both she and Margaret contributed many insights into her parents' attitudes and personality and described a lifestyle that, it is sad to say, has all but disappeared from the American scene:

> Our parents were deeply religious people and saw to it that we went to church every Sunday regardless of the weather, said Clara. In the winter, we took warm bricks to put under our feet while we rode to church in a horse-drawn spring wagon.

The Schnebly Family *in Gorin, Mo., 1907.*

Ellsworth age seven and Genivieve two,
taken five months after Pearl's death, 1905.

Photos courtesy of Paula Schnebly Hokanson

Mother and dad were very caring parents and did all they could to make us happy. They were a congenial couple and I personally never remember cross words between them. Margaret reminded me that now and then mother did get provoked with dad, particularly when he got into arguements about religion or politics. On those occasions she threatened to go live in the barn. I never understood why she wanted to go to the barn when our house was so nice.

People were always welcomed into our home, even strangers and if the strangers needed a meal or a place to sleep for the night, our folks provided this for them.

Mother made all of our clothes and dad made new soles for our shoes when they wore out. We each had two pairs of shoes. One for school and one for church.

I never knew where money came from except there was some in a cup in the cupboard which we used for stamps, or other incidentals, but we never had any for anything else.

Mother made candy for us like fudge, divinity and taffy, but I thought store-bought candy was a real treat. It always disturbed me when dad took eggs and cream to the grocery store and traded them for groceries we needed. That way he never owed a bill. Most of the neighbors charged their groceries and when they paid their bill, the grocer gave them a bag of candy to take to their children. Dad never got one and that upset me.

Dad forbade dancing, drinking and card playing. He said that if you went to dances there was always drinking and if you drank, it led to gambling. He did allow some card games such as Authors and Flinch, which we played as a family on Sundays or on bad weather days.

Our folks loved to celebrate holidays. At Easter we had scads of colored eggs that we would hunt all day. On the Fourth of July there were plenty of fire crackers, rockets, sparklers, lemonade and homemade ice cream. On Valentine's Day we made our own Valentines using wall paper samples with pretty flowers which we cut from seed catalogs and used to decorate our valentines.

Of course Thanksgiving and Christmas were very special with a big turkey dinner and a house full of guests.

Even though we had little rain in Boyero and hailstorms often destroyed our crops just before harvest time, I never heard dad complain. If a big hailstorm ruined the crops, dad would send us out with buckets after it was over and we would collect hailstones and mother made ice cream with them.

Dad depended on the Farmer's Almanac for just about everything regarding farming. Most chores had to be done according to certain phases of the moon such as planting crops, weaning calves, putting eggs under setting hens and hoeing weeds in the garden. I always wished we would lose that almanac around the time we had to hoe weeds.

We raised lots of watermelons and dad was very strict about when we could pick them. We children couldn't wait lots of times, so we would go out and pick one and then have to bury the rinds so dad wouldn't find out. Many times, just as the watermelons were ripe, a hailstorm would come and burst the watermelons. When that happened, dad would alert the neighbors to come and get all they wanted of the busted watermelons. What the neighbors didn't want the pigs and coyotes finished up. Coyotes love watermelons.

Margaret remembered their father's 'hot beds,' which were large holes facing south near her mother's wash house. Deep layers of manure were put into the holes beneath the soil where seeds were planted.

On sunny winter days, the hot beds were uncovered to attract the light and warmth. Whenever a hailstorm destroyed dad's crops, he would replant them with the sprouts from the hot bed.

I recall one bad hailstorm in late May when Clara and I were sent out to round up the baby chicks and turkeys. We wore ten pound buckets on our heads to protect us. The noise was deafening and our arms were black and blue when it was over. But we didn't have any lumps on our heads.

Clara and Margaret also recalled that box socials were a favorite community activity and every Sunday after church, families took turns hosting dinners to which everyone in the congregation was invited. When she graduated from high school, Clara was the only one in her graduating class. "I can have a class reunion whenever I want one," she said.

Shortly after Clara graduated from high school, a set of circumstances occurred which allowed her parents to return to Arizona and to the town they helped establish.

In January of 1931, during the height of the Great Depression, Sedona's mother, Amanda, had a deadly stroke. Sedona hurried to Gorin to care for her, but didn't arrive in time. Amanda Miller died with little left to her name, having lost everything when the Gorin bank closed down after the 'Crash.'

That same month, Carl faced one of the fiercest blizzards of the decade. He lost most of his cattle in the storm. In addition, he came down with the influenza, which was sweeping the country. For the first time in his life, Carl Schnebly took to his bed. By summer, Carl's remaining cattle broke out with the deadly anthrax disease, and Carl was forced to stay up day and night for weeks burning their carcasses, and the ground where they died, with yucca weeds. This was the only way to prevent the disease from seeping into the ground water and watering ponds. By fall, more cattle died from eating corn stalks poisoned by an early frost. Exhausted, discouraged and in poor health, Carl was forced to seek a doctor. The doctor told him he must go to a warmer, drier climate immediately or his health might be permanently impaired.

Carl sold what was left of his stock and his farm and moved the family to Phoenix where his brother William now lived. His brother Elsworth already had died in Phoenix in 1920, following an unsuccessful operation.

After three months in Phoenix, Carl couldn't resist the urge to move to Sedona, even though he'd been warned to avoid higher altitudes. Carl's old friends the Farleys (who were the first people Carl had met when he came to Arizona in 1901 and who had convinced him his possessions would be safe on the mountainside), offered him a job on their farm. So at the age of 68, Carl gratefully accepted their offer to work as a farm hand for $30 a month.

Despite his doctor's warning, Carl's health improved and he knew he would never leave Sedona again. By then there no longer was any trace of their original home, except little Pearl's grave. It was still on the land owned now by the Blacks. Carl got permission from the Cook family to move her remains to their family cemetery located off the present Airport Road. Carl carried Pearl's remains himself, and re-buried her in her present resting ground.

The Schneblys moved into a one-room frame house off the present Jordan Road and settled back into the life of their small community.

Margaret milked a cow each day for the Farleys in order to contribute a quart of milk to the family needs. Sedona washed and ironed the uniforms of the CCC (Civilian Conservation Corps) boys who worked on government jobs in and around Flagstaff and Sedona.

"Mother didn't have a washing machine," recalls Margaret. "She scrubbed those uniforms on a wash board all day, and then ironed them into the night." For this, Sedona earned about 10 cents a shirt.

Mr. Farley, who was a good carpenter, added some rooms to their little house. After Sedona stuffed newspapers and batting into the cracks to give their home more warmth, she covered the rough boards with blue and pink 'building paper.'

Then Ruth and Walter Jordan, a young couple who had taken over running the elder Jordan's fruit orchards along with their in-laws, Helen and George Jordan, hired all three Schneblys to work for them. Margaret picked fruit during harvest, Carl worked in the orchards and Sedona cleaned house, cooked, canned fruit and helped care for the Walter Jordans' three small children.

Helen Jordan reminisced about the effect of the depression on Sedona farmers in the Westerner's book, THOSE WERE THE DAYS.

> During the Depression, farm prices reached a new low, and with each farmer trying to compete with the other to sell produce that you could hardly give away, the farmers finally decided to form a cooperative. They brought their produce to our packing shed where we packed it uniformly. George did the marketing for everyone. He made regular trips each week to Cottonwood, Clarkdale, Jerome, Prescott, Flagstaff, Williams, Ashfork, Williams and Holbrook and overnight trips to Phoenix. He would get home late from these trips and we would work till midnight getting the truck loaded for the next trip the following day. Seemed like George never went to bed. He'd come in after I went to bed, take off his pants, shake them out, put them back on and head for Flagstaff.

With donated effort, the Jordans' canvas-sided packing shed soon became a packing house which today still serves the community as the Sedona Arts Center.

In the meantime, with so much grueling work to be done at the Jordan farm, especially after the fall harvest, the young Jordans relied more and more on the hard-working, experienced Schneblys. In time, a strong bond and lasting friendship developed between the two couples.

Sedona, or Aunt Dona as she was affectionately called, not only endeared herself to the Jordans but to the small community as well. Aunt Dona always had a cookie jar filled with fresh

Golden
Wedding
Anniversary,
1947

Photos courtesy of Paula Schnebly Hokanson

Carl Schnebly, *1953*

Carl and Dona *in front of Sedona's old
school house which later burned, 1940's.*

baked goods for the many children who loved to visit her. She and
the Jordans were active in the American Union Sunday School.
Aunt Dona put herself whole-heatedly into the group, serving as
their secretary-treasurer. She invested the Sunday school savings
into bonds, and the group looked forward to the day when they
could build a chapel where people of all denominations might
worship. When the old school house, where they met, mysteriously
burned down, the Assembly of God church offered their building
for the use of the group. Finally, as their building fund grew, thanks
to Sedona's careful investments, the Wayside Chapel was built on
land donated by the Jordan family.

It was about this time, following World War II, that Hwy. 89A
was completed through Oak Creek Canyon, and the first major
influx of tourists began to discover the scenic wonders of the little
town. Many bought property and returned later to retire. Artists,
writers and other talented individuals also looked upon Sedona as
the "Shangri-la of the West," and the community that Carl and
Sedona helped found took on a unique personality of its own.

On February 24, 1947, Carl and Sedona celebrated their 50th wedding anniversary, and the entire community turned out to pay them homage as did old friends who traveled miles to join in the celebration. Three years later, just before the Wayside Chapel was to be dedicated on April 5, 1950, Aunt Dona was taken to the hospital for major surgery. She returned home in time for the dedication, but one month later was back in the hospital again. Carl was told that Sedona had cancer and that she only had a few months to live.

Carl disregarded the doctor's suggestion that Sedona not be told. He was no good at keeping secrets from his beloved companion of 53 years. Sedona accepted the news stoically and with her usual courage. "Everyone has to go sometime," she said, "and I'm ready."

Carl stayed constantly at Sedona's bedside, never leaving for more than a few minutes. Friends who paid daily visits were always greeted with her warm and cheerful smile.

On Sunday, November 12, 1951 the minister came to give Sedona communion. Many of her family members were at her bedside and shared in the communion ceremony. Sedona knew her time was near. She asked those present to tell everyone that rather than send flowers to her funeral, would they instead contribute to a bell for the new chapel she had helped to found. That night, the doctor, friends and family stayed with her. By 10 a.m. of the following day, Sedona Arabella Miller Schnebly died on November 13, surrounded by those she loved. She was laid to rest at the Cook family cemetery beside her darling Pearl.

Within a month, the fund for the bell for Sedona had grown substantially, fed by friends and the numerous passing tourists. Sedona's son Hank found a bell in Denver, Colorado. After a belfry was constructed by Carl and others, the new bell was hung on Christmas Eve. A bronze plate set in the wall below the belfry read:

THE WAYSIDE CHAPEL BELL
DEDICATED
IN LOVING MEMORY OF
SEDONA M. SCHNEBLY

On Mother's Day, 1951, every seat of the chapel was filled as the pastor recounted Sedona Schnebly's life story. At the end of the service, the congregation joined hands as the new bell was dedicated to the mother of the town. Carl and his son Elsworth pulled the rope together, giving the bell a voice that resounded throughout the red rock canyons Sedona M. Schnebly had grown to love so much.

Two years later, on another Mother's Day an organ also was donated in her memory. It was the last Mother's Day Carl would know. He was found slumped over his washing machine, where on March 13, 1954, he quietly slipped away at the age of 86 to join his precious lady.

Chapter Five

ANYTHING IS POSSIBLE WITH FAITH
Nassan Gobran Helps Sedona
Become An Arts Community

wise soul once observed "God may have done some fine work in the Grand Canyon, but He prefers to live in Sedona"...and wherever God lives, artists follow.

Since the 1940's, hundreds of artists have called Sedona home, from the internationally renowned to the Sunday dabbler. Sedona inspires artistic endeavors. No one was more aware of this than Nassan Abiskhairoun Gobran, a renowned Egyptian artist who arrived in Sedona in 1950. Because of him, Sedona's establishment as an arts community was initiated.

Nassan Gobran was teaching fine arts at the Boston Museum in Massachusetts when Hamilton Warren, founder of Sedona's famous Verde Valley School, invited him to Sedona to establish an art department. Warren wrote to Gobran, and later arrived in Boston with photographs of Sedona. Sedona in the late 1940's was a place most people including Gobran, had never heard of before. At first Gobran was not interested in Warren's invitation. It was the movie, BROKEN ARROW, which changed his mind.

"The night after Hamilton Warren left Boston, I went to see BROKEN ARROW with some of my friends," recalled Gobran."To my surprise, the movie was filmed in the very place Hamilton Warren had shown me photographs of the night before. So I said to myself, 'God must want me to go there.'" Nassan made up his mind, however, he would stay only one year.

When Gobran arrived in Sedona, there were about 350 people living here. Like so many artists before and since Gobran's arrival, his first view of Sedona's remarkable landscape left him stunned. Gobran realized that Sedona was a place where the arts would flourish.

Nassan A. Gobran's own artistic career began at an early age. When he was twelve, he spent his first earnings on buckets of clay from the banks of the Nile. On the roof of his father's house in Cairo, he modeled his versions of Egyptian mythology and farm life. In 1931, he enrolled in the Cairo Fine Arts School, where he

Max Ernst and Dorathea Tanning, *1953. This famous artist couple pose at their Sedona home with CAPRICORN. Ernst, an internationally acclaimed surrealist, was one of the founders of the DADA movement in France. Photo courtesy of Luiz Schlesinger*

graduated with high honors after four years. One year later, he entered what was then called the Royal College of Fine Arts of Cairo University. There he received recognition from the Egyptian Ministry of Education, who bought two of his works to represent contemporary Egyptian sculpture in the International Exhibition in Paris.

Despite the fact that Nassan was a Coptic Christian and not a Moslem, he received grants from the Ministry of Education from 1943 to 1946 to study architecture, sculpture and heiroglyphs in the temple at Luxor. He also continued to make commissioned works for the Royal family, the Ministries of Agriculture and Education, the Royal Opera, and the Civilization Museum.

During the Second World War, numerous Americans visited Nassan's studio in Cairo, from soldiers to scientists, to American Embassy staff members. All urged him to come to America, and some even used their influence to recommend him to various schools. Many teaching fellowship offers followed. The one Nassan finally chose was at the Boston Museum School of Fine Arts.

During the summer of 1948, Nassan was appointed by Serge Koussevitsky and Boris Goldovsky to head the scenic department of the Berkshire Music Festival at Tanglewood. His first assignment was to design sets for the American premiere of Rossini's opera, "THE TURK IN ITALY."

From the time he arrived in America, Nassan's progress had been watched closely by Gretchen Warren, a prominent and wealthy Boston citizen, and a member of the board at the Boston Museum School of Fine Arts. She also was the mother of Hamilton Warren, who had founded Sedona's Verde Valley School in 1948. She urged her son to invite the young sculptor to head up the school's art department, which Warren proceeded to do.

Shortly after Gobran arrived in Sedona, he met other artists living in here: Cowboy artists John Hampton and Charlie Dye, and the internationally famous surrealist, Max Ernst and his wife, artist Dorathea Tanning.

German born Max Ernst had helped found the Dada movement of art in Cologne. He was one of the originators of collages using photographs of non-related subjects, unified by gouache and ink pencil. His work inspired Andre Breton, the future leader of Surrealism. Ernst's collages, though under the banner of Dada, were among those works which heralded Surrealism.

In 1930, Ernst was associated with Salvador Dali in the production of the film, "L'age d'or," and in 1934, he participated with Joan Miro in an exhibition in Zurich entitled "WHAT IS SURREALISM?" In 1941, he escaped the Nazi's with the help of Peggy Guggenheim, who got him to America. While in California, he met Dorathea Tanning. The couple were married in 1946 and shortly afterwards, settled in Sedona. It was in Sedona that Ernst would create his world famous sculpture "Capricorn."

The Ernsts were living on Brewer Road when Nassan met them. After the couple left Sedona in 1953 to live in France, Nassan rented their home and studio. In 1960, Ernst commissioned Nassan to make a duplicate model of his famous sculpture CAPRICORN. The original, created in cement at his Brewer Road home, could not be moved. It was a long and arduous job, but eventually the model was shipped to Paris, where castings were made in bronze for world wide distribution to museums.

Needless to say, Gobran by now had decided to remain in Sedona. He already had made up his mind as well to start an arts center here.

Model For Capricorn By Max Ernst, *1960, Nassan Gobran prepares the first mold for world-famous surrealist Max Ernst's CAPRICORN, copies of which are in Museum collections around the world. Photo courtesy of Luiz Schlesinger*

"I traveled to The Museum of Northern Arizona and to Flagstaff Teacher's College, now Northern Arizona University, to discuss the idea of forming an arts center here." said Gobran. "No one seemed interested in pursuing the idea with me, and one even tried to discourage me entirely. "Sedona is a dead-end place," one even went so far as to say, "nothing will ever happen there." Fortunately for Sedona, Gobran remained determined to follow through with his dream.

By 1953, Gobran had resigned his post at the Verde Valley School in order to devote more time to his own art. One day, Dr. Harry Woods, chairman of the art department at Arizona State University, visited Gobran. By the time he left, Gobran had convinced Woods to initiate a summer graduate arts school in Sedona. In 1956, the first classes were held at the Kings Ransom Motel (now Quality Inn) and by the following year, at Sedona's elementary school. Teachers and art supervisors from 28 states attended the summer sessions, and Gobran's dream of establishing an arts center in Sedona moved closer to reality. The classes continued each summer until 1961.

Inspired by the enthusiastic response to the summer art classes, Gobran took the next step toward his dream. He invited a group of prominent area people to a dinner, which he prepared himself. The group included George Babbitt, uncle to Bruce Babbitt, 1988 Presidential hopeful; Hamilton and Barbara Warren, founders of the Verde Valley School; Tony and Marguerite Staude, founders of the Chapel of the Holy Cross; Bill Leenhouts, lawyer and rancher; Douglas and Elizabeth Rigby, well-known authors; Eugenia Wright, donor of land for the original Sedona Library; William Stevenson, attorney, Helen Varner Frye, landowner; Cecil J. Lockhart-Smith, Sedona businessman; and Cowboy artist John Hampton.

Gobran poured out his hopes and dreams to them of starting an arts center in Sedona. He asked each if they would serve on the first board of directors.

Everyone agreed to serve, and contributed $30 a-piece to get things rolling. Because Gobran's English was still so poor, the group elected George Babbitt as their first president. Incorporation papers were drawn up establishing the Canyon Kiva Arts Center. The papers were signed in 1958, the same year Gobran celebrated his U.S. citizenship. Then a year went by and nothing more happened in regards to the new arts center.

"I finally called George Babbitt," said Gobran. "He confessed he was too busy to follow through, and asked to resign from the board. I pleaded with him to stay, but he just wasn't interested." With Babbitt's resignation, Nassan became President, Barbara Warren, vice-president and Cecil Lockhart-Smith, secretary and treasurer.

Shortly after his discouraging conversation with Babbitt, Gobran was in Cecil Lockhart-Smith's Saddle Rock arts supply store when he overheard a conversation between Cecil and the president of the Sedona Chamber of Commerce, Ray Comerford. Comerford was telling Cecil that the chamber was looking for a project that would help Sedona become known.

"I ran into the back room and told him that I had something unusual to suggest," recalled Gobran. Comerford listened to what Gobran had to say and then invited him to share his idea at the next chamber meeting.

Attentive chamber members were impressed as they listened to Gobran's broken, but eloquent English as he poured out his idea of establishing an arts center in Sedona. One member, Bud Hummel, called Gobran the next day. Hummel owned land that included the old wooden apple-packing barn that stood at the end of the vast Jordan Farm and the old Jordan home. He generously

Sedona Arts Center, *1961.*

Rags To Riches Ball, *1974. One of Sedona's most popular social events. This was an annual costume ball at the Sedona Arts Center which used varying themes throughout the years.*

Photos courtesy of Elizabeth Rigby

Sedona Jazz Festival, *1982. Johnny Gilbert rehearses for Sedona's first jazz festival which was held at the Sedona Arts Center. The resounding success of this concert inspired Gilbert and others to establish the nationally known JAZZ ON THE ROCKS FESTIVAL held annually in Sedona each September, and always sold out months in advance.*

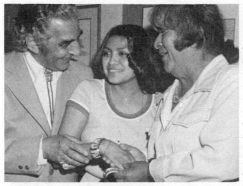

Breaking With Tradition, *1978.*
*Charles Loloma, internationally
renowned Hopi artist and jewelry
designer, and his niece Verme
Nequatewa, show Loloma's
tradition-breaking jewelry designs
to Nassan Gobran. These in-
novative designs, which would
bring international acclaim to the
artist, were envisioned after
Loloma's visit to Egypt with
Gobran. His niece, Verma, also
would become a leader in jewelry
design within a few years after this
photo was taken.*

Five-Man Show, *1979. Frank McCarthy (left), famous Cowboy Artist and Sedona
resident chats with well-known wildlife artist, Don Rodell.*

Five-Man Show, *1979. Two of Sedona's
most famous resident artists, Joe Beeler
and James Reynolds, shared the spotlight
for this well-attended and well-remembered
show at SAC which also featured Frank
McCarthy, John Hampton, and George
Phippin.*

Photos courtesy of Elizabeth Rigby

The Barry Goldwaters, *1971.
Senator Barry Goldwater and his
wife Peggy were among the Sedona
Arts Center's early supporters. Here
they receive tickets to a gourmet
dinner from SAC founder, Nassan
Gobran.*

offered the barn as the first headquarters for the proposed arts center at a rent of $25 a month. The house on the property was leased for $75 a month. Hummel said he would sell both properties to the arts center for $35,000.

The barn had been abandoned for many years. Tar paper hung off the walls and the ceilings looked as if they might collapse any day. But to Gobran, the old barn was brimming with possibilities.

With a group of volunteers, Gobran set to work renovating the barn. Before eight months had passed, the apple packing stalls had become departments for painting, sculpture, mosaics, ceramics, and creative writing. The Chamber of Commerce voted to pay the first year's rent on the structure and on April 28, 1961, the Jordan apple barn, now known as the Sedona Arts Center, held its grand opening show. The opening show featured works by Max Ernst and Dorathea Tanning, and by a well-known Arizona artist, Lew Davis.

Over 300 people arrived to see the show and hear a concert by Victor Lombardi's 50 piece orchestra. "We were able to acquire this famous orchestra at very little cost because Hamilton Warren had accidentally booked them to perform at his school on the same night he had booked a choir," said Gobran.

Almost everyone who attended the gala opening signed up as the center's charter members. Seven years later, the barn's $35,000 mortgage was burned. The money came from generous donations, dinner dances, art shows, musical performances and classes.

Gobran, and other board members like Al Nestler, a nationally recognized landscape artist who opened Sedona's first art gallery, not only taught classes and donated their fees to the mortgage fund, but helped cook gourmet meals with other board members. Everyone on the board donated time, money and ingredients to these well-attended dinner parties. Gobran gives particular credit for the success of the Sedona Arts Center to Cecil Lockhart-Smith and Maude Harmon. "They worked harder than anyone," he said. "Without their help, I don't think we would have made it." Cecil served as president of the arts center for eight years, and Maude was vice-president and chairman of exhibitions for ten years.

As the population of Sedona doubled and re-doubled, 'The Barn,' as it was affectionately known, became the hub of all the social and cultural activity in the community. Eventually a stage and lower gallery were added with a minimal cost due to maximum volunteer labor. Once this mortgage was burned, Gobran relinquished his involvement to others, and returned to his own, highly successful, artistic career.

By 1986, Sedona boasted over 30 art galleries, and the Sedona Arts Center hired its first professional arts director, Marilyn Nicholson. She was on hand to help the center celebrate its 25th anniversary on April 28, 1986. Many of the original charter members returned, as did Victor Lombardi's band.

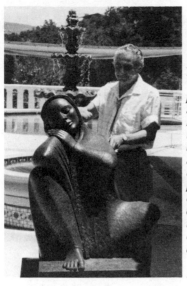

Nassan Gobran With 'Peace' (Bronze), *1989.* *This bronze, which sits in the patio of a private Sedona home, was first carved in stone and then bronze-cast in New York. Nassan prefers to directly carve on the stone rather than use pneumatic tools. This, he believes, is the true path to the art of the sculptor. "Stone is a sensuous material," he explains. "Each area of the stone has its particular live quality, its own spirit. It is only while carving that the sculptor discovers this spirit. When the two spirits - the sculptor's and the stone's - merge into oneness, they create a new spiritual entity able to live forever in its own right."*

Photo by Kate Ruland-Thorne

Since Nicholson's arrival, the arts center's membership has grown from 700 members to over 2,000. The center attracts prestigious national traveling shows and remains the hub of Sedona's arts and social activities.

Nassan Gobran, like so many of Sedona's professional artists, continues to live, work and remain continually inspired by 'God's dwelling place.' One only has to witness the intensity of colors, the dramatic skies, the sculptured formations and the sun's romantic caress of the red rocks at the beginning and end of each day, to understand why so many artists have flocked here. Yet the creative ones will tell you there is more.

Often 'that more' is explained as an energy, something powerful and mysterious, which brings forth their most inspired ideas for novels, sculpture, musical scores, the dance, designs, photography, acting, inventions or fine paintings. Whatever their reasons for coming are, Sedona has drawn hundreds of creative people to its bosom for nearly half-a-century. Over 300 professional artists presently call Sedona home.

Nassan continues to sculpt, and is one of the only artists who uses only stone native to Arizona in his work. In addition to onyx, his favorite, he works in Arizona granite, quartzite, copper ore, lapis lazuli and bronze. His work is found in museums and public and private collections around the world, and he has been listed in WHO'S WHO OF AMERICAN ART since 1958.

Whatever Sedona has given to him, Gobran has returned one-hundred-fold. His own words as to how Sedona became an arts community describe it best: "Anything is possible when you have faith."

Chapter Six

JOE BEELER AND THE COWBOY
ARTISTS OF AMERICA

oe and Sharon Beeler scraped together every cent they had to move to Sedona, Arizona in 1961. The couple had discovered Sedona two years before, while attending a Western Writer's of America conference in Tucson. On the way home, they drove through red rock country and immediately knew they would move here as soon as they could afford it.

At the beginning of the 1960's, Joe Beeler's career as an artist looked promising. His work was displayed regularly in a prominent Arizona gallery, O'Brian's Art Emporium in Phoenix; he was illustrating books for the University of Oklahoma Press; additional covers for the CATTLEMAN'S magazine were planned using his art; and he had two prestigious exhibitions under his belt, one in Albuquerque and one at the Gilcrease Institute in Tulsa, Oklahoma. Walter Bimson, the Dean of American art collectors, had acquired one of Joe's paintings, and another prominent art patron, W.B. Davis, had purchased Joe's work for the permanent collection at the Gilcrease Institute.

But all of this growing success and recognition was not creating a surplus in the Beelers' bank account. A major part of the problem was where the Beelers lived. The Beeler cabin at Five Mile Creek in northern Oklahoma was not exactly a place where people lined up to buy art.

Joe's art career had succeeded this far because he wasn't afraid to hustle. His country-boy personality and his ability to saddle his own horse, or rope and drag calves to a branding fire, made ranch folks welcome him wherever he went. Often they would commission him to paint their prize bull or horse. After he was paid on those occasions, the Beelers ate hamburger instead of rabbit or venison, which Joe's sharp aim with a rifle or six-shooter helped keep as a staple on their table.

In 1961, Joe was invited to exhibit his paintings at the Western Writer's of America annual meeting, to be held this time in Elko, Nevada. Joe was particularly excited about this opportunity because

Joe Beeler in his Sedona Studio, *1989. Photo by Kate Ruland-Thorne*

a representative from a New York Publishing house, Grosset and Dunlap, was attending the conference and wanted to discuss with Joe the possibility of illustrating books for the company. If he landed this job, he and Sharon believed they might afford their long-awaited move to Sedona. Joe met Mr. Svenson the editor and his wife at the Elko Airport and drove them out to the ranch for a barbecue.

Joe was nervous about making a good impression on the Svensons. It was the first time the couple had ever been out west, and they were delighted by the wide open spaces and this young cowboy artist's western attire and Oklahoma drawl.

The car bounced along a ranch road and soon approached a stock tank with seven jack rabbits sitting around it. On impulse, Joe drew out his six-shooter and started firing. For a moment all he thought about was food for the table, not his passengers. As soon as Joe started to blaze away through the rolled-down car window, Mrs. Svenson screamed. Joe realized too late he had thrown the couple into a panic. In his frustration and embarrassment, he pulled the still-cocked pistol inside the car and accidentally fired another shot, which shattered the windshield. Mrs. Svenson screamed again and threw herself across her husband's lap and half-way out the window. Joe said he probably would have shot himself by then if there had been any more shells left in the pistol. He had never felt worse in his life.

But the incident became a highlight in the history of the Western Writer's organization. After the Svensons calmed down, they enjoyed the prospect of taking a real western story home with them, complete with smoking guns. Joe also was awarded the illustrating job.

With an illustrating job assured and another exhibition in the works at the Montana Historical Society, Sharon and Joe believed they could finally afford to move to Arizona. They decided they would use the money from the sales at the Montana show to get them here.

The Beelers made the long drive to Helena, Montana, and checked into a cheap motel. The show at the historical society hung for a month. Not one painting sold. The Beelers glumly faced the possibility that they might be stuck in Oklahoma, perhaps forever.

On the last day of the show, five paintings sold. Full of renewed optimism and a healthy confidence in their future, the Beelers finally arrived in Sedona, Arizona.

In Sedona, Joe Beeler's artistic career would soar. Three other successful professional Arizona artists became his good friends and encouraged Joe in his own ambitions. They were Charlie Dye, John Hampton and George Phippin. Phippin also helped Joe get started as a sculptor. All four of them not only enjoyed each other's company, but were interested in Western subjects, and each felt more at home in a round-up camp than at a tea party. When Joe looks back on the many turning points in his career, he will readily tell you that moving to Sedona, and becoming friends with these three artists, were among the most significant:

> We had just barely scraped together everything we had to move out here, and we hadn't been here but a few weeks when Al Nestler, who owned the first gallery in Sedona, sold one of my paintings for $1,000. It was the most money I had ever received for a painting. Suddenly we could pay the rent.
>
> Sedona was becoming the hub of many artists' gatherings by the time we arrived. Everything revolved around either the Sedona Arts Center or our home. An awful lot of artists came through here and we would have a dinner party at the drop of a hat. Our home became a gathering place for such artists as Olaf Weighorst, Charlie Dye, John Hampton, "Shorty" Shope, Gordon Snidow, Grant Speed, George Phippin...you name it.
>
> Western writer Bob McLeod (who wrote APPALOOSA which starred Marlon Brando in the film version) lived here with his wife, Laurie. He knew how to play the guitar and played at all of our gatherings. Our children, Tracy and Jody, grew up around some really interesting people.

In November of 1964, three years after he arrived in Sedona, Joe went on a trip to a large "rancho" in Sonora, Mexico, with Charlie Dye and John Hampton. They had such a great time, that on the way home they began to kick around the idea of organizing an informal group of men who, like themselves, found pleasure in the saddle as well as at the easel.

Cowboy Artists of America *organizational meeting at the Oak Creek Tavern, June 23, 1965. From left, Joe Beeler, 1931; Charlie Dye, 1906-1973; John Hampton, 1918; Robert MacLeod, 1906: MacLeod played an important role in organizing the group, but because he devoted more time to writing than painting, he became the organization's first associate member. Photo by Elizabeth Rigby*

By the following summer, the idea had taken root as more and more of their artist friends showed enthusiasm for the idea. Hampton, Beeler, Dye, writer Bob McLeod and George Phippin met one night at the Oak Creek Tavern in Sedona, and over a few beers, founded the Cowboy Artists of America on June 23, 1965. Phippin was named President; Dye, Vice-President; Hampton, Secretary; and Beeler, Treasurer. Later they adopted by-laws and a constitution. Their goals were as follows:

> To perpetuate the memory and culture of the Old West as typified by the late Frederic Remington, Charles Russell, and others; to insure authentic representation of the life of the West, as it was and is, to maintain standards of quality in contemporary Western painting, drawing, and sculpture; to help guide collectors of Western art; to give mutual assistance in the protection of artists' rights; to conduct a trail ride and camp out in some locality of special interest each year; and to hold a joint exhibition of the work of active members, once a year.

Within a very short time, the Cowboy Artists of America would grow into one of the most influential forces and dramatic success stories in the history of American art.

Featured Artists at Sedona Arts Center, *1965. Charlie Dye with Sharon Beeler, Joe Beeler and Dye's wife Mary during opening exhibit of the men's work. Photo by Elizabeth Rigby*

Three months after forming the Cowboy Artists (CA), Joe was invited to have a one-man show at the newly opened National Cowboy Hall of Fame and Western Heritage Center in Oklahoma City. His would be the first full-fledged exhibition by a living artist at the National Cowboy Hall of Fame - a real distinction. This show, along with the one at the Montana Historical Society and the Gilcrease Institute, gave Joe's art an exposure no other living western painter had ever received.

During this exhibition, Joe told Dean Krakel, the founding director of the Cowboy Hall of Fame, and the Hall's art director, Jim Boren, about the newly formed CA organization. Boren and Krakel promptly invited the CA to present their first exhibition at the Cowboy Hall of Fame the following year.

The CA's first show opened September 9, 1966, and ran through October 16. Joe and twelve other members brought their work to Oklahoma City, very apprehensive about how the public would respond.

The artists, besides Joe, whose work was shown were: Charlie Dye, John Hampton, Fred Harmon, Darol Dickinson, Wayne Hunt, Harvey Johnson, John Kittelson, George Marks, "Shorty Shope," Gordon Snidow, Grant Speed, and Byron Wolfe. George Phippin had died earlier in the year. Almost $50,000 worth of art was sold during the show, and the Cowboy Hall of Fame invited them back the following year.

Joe Beeler, 1989 *Photo by Kate Ruland-Thorne*

Joe Beeler was 35 years old at the time of his first CA show, and already he had achieved more success than most artists achieve in a life-time. His art was in such demand that he could hardly keep up with it. Both he and Sharon agreed that it was a lot harder to cope with success then with poverty. But they were very proud of the fact that Joe's art was rapidly becoming recognized not only for its historic value, but because each one was an excellent example of fine art.

At the 1967 CA show, Joe's bronze sculpture SIOUX was selected as the show's outstanding sculpture, and a few months later he presented a one-man show at the prestigious Heard Museum in Phoenix. The most dramatic highlight of 1967 was the fall publication by the University of Oklahoma Press of Joe's art called "COWBOYS AND INDIANS: Characters in Oil and Bronze." It was the first book to be done on a contemporary Western artist.

In 1968, Joe was elected president of the Cowboy Artists of America, whose membership had grown to 25. The public's response to the annual show and to the work of its individual members was phenomenal. In Joe's words, "Cowboy art was going at a high lope and showing no signs of tiring."

In 1973, the Cowboy Artists of America moved their show to the Phoenix Art Museum. In 1990, they will celebrate their 25th anniversary. Today, thousands of people from around the world attend the show with sales going well over the one million mark annually.

Jody Beeler
at his video
studio.

Sharon Beeler

Tracy Beeler

*Photos by
Kate Ruland-Thorne, 1989.*

"You know, none of us had any idea that what we started in Sedona would grow into what it is today," said Joe. "In fact you could say that we (artists) have grown together, too. We're like family. Even our kids grew up together."

Today Joe continues to sculpt and paint in his Sedona studio, surrounded by memorabilia and artifacts of the old West. He never misses an opportunity to climb on his horse and enter roping contests for charity. His daughter Tracy shares the studio with him and is becoming an excellent bronze sculptor in her own right. Sharon too, has entered into the world of art. She has earned recognition for her brilliant landscapes and colorful floral subjects. Perhaps writer Ben K. Green, whose books often were illustrated by Joe, best sums up his character and his legacy to the arts:

> Joe Beeler has worked hard all of his life at trying to make a reputation as an artist and a cowhand. Well, the fine old artists say that he ought to be a good cowhand, and the cowhands say he sure ought to be a good artist. The fact of the matter is, he is still working hard at both and when you come down to the facts, his paintbrush hand has been rope-burned and his art shows it in a fresh authentic way. He has worked in oil, watercolor and bronze and has earned recognition in all. Joe is a good fellow to meet and pass the time of day with and has contributed more than one man's share in preserving the old West in art.

Chapter Seven

"UPON THIS ROCK..."
*Marguerite Staude and the
Chapel of the Holy Cross*

woman slipped into the cool, dimly lit sanctuary of the Chapel of the Holy Cross and sat down near the entrance. No one else seemed present. Soon the chapel doors would be locked for the night.

Beyond the cathedral window behind the altar, the last rays of the sun illuminated the red rocks outside. Within the chapel, the only other light was from candles flickering in multicolored glass containers along the walls. It was a rare moment of solitude for the woman. She folded her hands on her lap, closed her eyes, and absorbed the peaceful, forgiving energy, which is forever present in this chapel of the desert.

Moments of perfect quiet passed before the woman heard someone stir near the altar. The shadowy figure of a man arose from the floor where he had been lying. The woman could not see the man's features until he passed her. He was young, disheveled and unshaven. A ragged backpack was slung over his shoulder. She glimpsed his face as he went by. Tears filled his intense blue eyes and streamed down his ruddy cheeks. Whatever it was this young man had sought within the Chapel of the Holy Cross. . .she could see that he had found it.

Marguerite Brunswig Staude, the creator of the Chapel of the Holy Cross, would have revered such a moment. "The doors of this chapel will ever be open to one and all, regardless of creed," she once wrote. "That this church may come to life in the souls of men and be a living reality...herein lies the whole message of this chapel."

Although born into wealth and privilege, Marguerite Staude never wavered from her belief that all mankind has need for a spiritual understanding. From the time she was a little girl, she spent most of her own life searching for God through art. As she often traveled the world, she always was drawn to, and collected, art that conveyed a strong spiritual message of beauty, interpretation and character. After she became a sculptor, painter and jewelry designer, Marguerite strived to capture the spirit within inert matter, and to bring it forth in her own creations. Her jewelry designs in particular, included the precious treasures she collected on her travels...beads from Ethiopia and Morocco, seal impressions from Mycenaean mythology or rattlesnake rattles and driftwood, gathered along the shore at her home in Big Sur. "Art is more than a clever arrangement of materials," she said. "For me, it is a search for the spiritual side of the universe."

Marguerite's father, Lucien Brunswig, came to America from France in the 1870's. He met and married her beautiful French Creole mother in New Orleans. There Marguerite was born on November 9, 1899, and named after her socially prominent mother. Marguerite was the youngest of five children.

By 1888, her father had founded the Brunswig Drug Company. Shortly after the turn-of-the century, the family moved to Los Angeles. Marguerite attended the Menlo Park Academy, a private girls' school located on the San Francisco Peninsula. When not in school, Marguerite often traveled the world with her mother, a woman she described as one with high ideals, an avid reader and fine writer.

While growing up, Marguerite always was drawing and painting. She soon shared with her mother a desire to find her own way in the world, and her own identity as an artist. After graduation, Marguerite decided she must go to Paris and study art, but first, she would have to break some ties with her socially prominent family.

On her father's birthday, she enclosed a note with her gift to him which read, "I prefer my liberty to the most beautiful gilded cage." Shortly afterwards, she left for Paris.

Paris in the 1920's was a paradise for artists and writers. It was the era of F. Scott Fitzgerald, Hemingway, Picasso and Modigliani. Marguerite studied with the great drama coach Yvette Gilbert and with artist Maria Wassilieff.

"Mademoiselle Gilbert opened the door to the world for me," said Marguerite. "She made me see behind the masks that people wear." Of Wassilieff, she said, "We studied the Cubists together. I could feel the sap coming out of her pencil as she drew. She knew how to capture thought and bring it to reality on paper."

Wassilieff, who had taught the great impressionist Modigliani, also brought to Marguerite's attention the exotic beauty of bronze, particularly the work coming out of West Africa at the time. It was Wassilieff who helped Marguerite settle on sculpture as her best means of expression. But it was to Gilbert that Marguerite gave the greatest credit. "My work with Yvette Gilbert," she wrote in 1987, "was the cornerstone of my entire artistic career."

After Marguerite left Paris, she traveled to Mexico City to study stone-carving with Carlos Bracho. Her first portrait bust was of him. It took the form of an Aztec mask, and suggested that her teacher was one with his culture. Many years later when the now famous Rain God was discovered in an Aztec ruin, it showed an uncanny resemblance to Marguerite's bust of Bracho.

By the 1930's, Marguerite was studying art in New York City. It was there that she first conceived the idea for what would one day evolve into the Chapel of the Holy Cross.

It was 1932, Ash Wednesday...the beginning of Lent, when all New York seemed to have congregated at St. Patrick's Cathedral to receive the ashes. I, too, with their seal on my brow, was heading my way out of the great Gothic Portals facing Rockefeller Center, which speaks so forceably of "today." I could not help but think, how come the Church clings to its past glory while seeming totally to ignore the present, as though it did not exist? After all, do we have no contemporary language by which to worship? Gothic is fine, but "Modern Gothic" speaks...or may I say, sings...so loudly today. These were my thoughts as we were headed out into the great modern structures of Rockefeller Center. Can there be no Church built to speak in contemporary language and opening into liturgical arts?

As Marguerite walked down The Avenues toward her apartment, her mind remained intent upon these questions, while her eyes absorbed all the new structures that she passed. Suddenly, there it was before her. None other than the Empire State Building, emerging out of its scaffolding. She saw a cross taking its form where the major vertical beam deliberately crosses the horizontal. Ah, she thought, just as the Gothic spirit overrides matter...this is the hidden strength it carries behind its own structure.

It was a thrilling thought, one that followed her and sang loudly in her being until she reached the penthouse apartment of her hotel on 85th Street. "After entering my apartment, I was struck by the views of this same 'Church.' It was like a dream; now a vision from afar. It illuminated itself. This image was to haunt me until the dream became a reality. And I must say, doors opened to make it so, as will be revealed."

Marguerite returned to her studio in California and created a model that captured her dream. After it was completed, she called her good friend, Jake Zietlin, of literary fame. After seeing the model, he put Marguerite in touch with Lloyd Wright, son of Frank Lloyd Wright, who called to see the model. That's when the idea really took fire.

As a project, we agreed to work out another model architecturally. He promised to respect my sculptural form. We worked at this project a full year, scanning plans of Gothic Cathedrals to bring the modern back to the classic background from whence it came.

79

Within a few months, the cruciform church in plan and elevation emerged. A most gratifying job during this time of the Depression. We had hoped to build it around the square block in Los Angeles, which was owned by the Catholic Church for its 'Cathedral of the Future.'

The plans involved a perforated doubled wall in tiny cement crosses. The whole structure would be lined with glass and the building would be done to a five hundred-foot scale. It formed its own natural beacon for airplanes, having its organic streamline plan follow through to the top cruciform from four angles - it would soar into space.

These details were illustrated in the inner cloisters as the site spread over one square block. The main entrance was to hold the Mystic Emblem of Christ. Other inner cloisters contained Our Lady's Chapel, The Chapel of the Old Law and the Chapel of the New Testament. Also, the stations of the cross came down the main isle of the interior of the Church and the Fifteen Mysteries of the Rosary spread in the background...all strong liturgical notes. The altar, in the center of the Church, was also cruciform following the basic form of the Church.

But alas, Marguerite was ahead of her time. The church officials had no interest in building such a "futuristic" structure. Their "Cathedral of the Future" would be built in the same manner as ones built in the past.

In 1937, their plans were accepted by the church in Budapest, Hungary. It was to be built on Mount Ghelert, one of the hills that overlooks the Danube. But the outbreak of World War II put an end to the idea, and Marguerite's Cathedral was shelved for the next twenty-five years.

She returned to Los Angeles, where she met her husband, Tony Staude. They were married on September 24, 1938. The Staudes' lives would revolve around the cultural and art circles in Los Angeles where Marguerite had made a name for herself as a sculptor. Her portraits in sculpture earned her awards, and included taking all honors in sculpture at the prestigious Los Angeles County Museum of Art exhibition.

After America became embroiled in World War II, Marguerite devoted herself to teaching wounded soldiers clay modeling as a therapy. Later, she also spent many years volunteering her time to teach the blind the same art.

From 1940 to 1960, the Staude family's vacations often were spent at their Doodlebug Ranch in Sedona, Arizona. Sedona was barely known in the early years of their visits. "We were about the only 'dudes' in town," recalled Marguerite.

By 1950, both of Marguerite's parents had died. After their death, a patrimony was established for a memorial in their name.

"It was my mother's last wish, that she not die without ful-
filling a living spiritual trust. That is when I decided to build a
Chapel in their memory, in the name and form of the cross. My
husband, Tony, and I had come to love Sedona, and we decided
that we would build our Chapel here in this red rock desert.
Instead of a Cathedral, our monument would become a Chapel
dedicated to finding God through art."

In the 1950's, an unusual chapel had been built in France,
designed by the painter Roualt for the purpose of finding God
through art. Marguerite was captivated by Roualt's personal hope
that this liturgical theme would create its own foundation both
spiritually and materially. She realized that this was the very
concept she desired for her own chapel. After returning to Los
Angeles, she immediately contacted Lloyd Wright. "We urged and
pleaded with him to work with us on our new idea," she said, "but
he refused, and clung to the original plans, which now were beyond
our reach financially."

A good friend of Marguerite's, sculptor Benny Buffano, contacted
architects Anshen and Allen of San Francisco and told them of
her Chapel. The architects made an appointment with the Staudes
to discuss the project. Marguerite recalled later that it was a special
situation where sculptor and architect met on common ground:

> After I explained my ideals to them, they were ready to
> be committed. Our pact was sealed. There were three
> members on our committee, Tony, myself and the architects.
> All of us were free to act independently as long as the action
> benefited and enhanced the good of the Chapel. We were much
> like a group of 'faithful' following our theme. The architects
> flew to Sedona, and I, too...terrified. Although it was 1955,
> I had never braved the air before. But, for such a high
> purpose, I decided one need not fear. Before we knew it, the
> desert stretched before us and we surveyed possible sites from
> the air.
>
> I was thrilled when we were finally able to step into a car
> and examine the sites that had presented themselves to us from
> the air. Though the possibilities were infinite, there was really
> only one site which cut itself out into space. We drove to this
> spur of rock which projected 200 feet above the desert floor.

Two strange and significant discoveries followed. Each one
convinced the Staudes that they had chosen the right place.

> At this site we had chosen, I discovered someone had carved
> an apothecary emblem in the rocks...the very emblem that
> was to back the whole project into being. Also, as I stood
> on this pinnacle and looked northeast, there stood the madonna
> and child, carved by nature into its nearly perfect form. Yes,

Marguerite Brunswig Staude, *1980*   *Photo courtesy of Tony Staude*

this was our site. Now we were set, all but for permits from
Church and State.

But as the Staudes soon were to learn, permission would not
come easily. When they flew to Gallup, New Mexico, to discuss
the Chapel with the Bishop of the Diocese, he tried to talk them
into allowing the church to build something more modest, giving
the remainder of the money to the Indians. Finally, he agreed he

Chapel of the Holy Cross, *1989.*
Photos by Kate Ruland-Thorne

The Madonna in the Rocks
looks toward the chapel.

Groundbreaking Ceremony, *1954. Father Driscoll of Cottonwood (second from left) prepares to bless the ground. Marguerite Staude stands near her car wearing a hat. Photo courtesy of Tony Staude*

could not refuse a gift, which this definitely was, and he gave his permission.

Since the site was on government land, Marguerite next traveled to Washington, D.C. Fortunately, Senator Barry Goldwater was their friend. "He was a great friend and admirer of this part of Arizona," said Marguerite. "He told us that Sedona could only be enhanced by this noble building to crown its crests. Had it not been for him, the Forestry Service would have taken years to come to any sort

Michael the Archangel *17th Century Mexican Colonial carved in wood.*

Tapestries are by Drouet, *a contemporary Polish artist.*

Saint Frances Memorial Fountain, *1989. Fountain designed by Bruno Groth in memory of Marguerite B. Staude.*

Sculpture by Marguerite B. Staude

Photos by Kate Ruland-Thorne

of decision. I thanked him profusely for so promptly obtaining a permit from the Department of Agriculture that allowed us to build upon these rocks."

In April of 1955, the William Simpson Construction Company broke ground. One year later, Marguerite's lifelong dream became a reality when the Chapel of the Holy Cross was completed.

Sculpture by
Marguerite B. Staude

Stations of the
Cross *Designed*
by Marguerite B.
Staude from
antique nails.

Sculptures by
Marguerite
B. Staude

Photos by Kate Ruland-Thorne

It has been over thirty years since the chapel was completed. From the beginning, this chapel in the desert, as Marguerite so fondly thought of it, has served as a place of inspiration for thousands of visitors each year. Among Marguerite's greatest treasures were letters people wrote to her about their feelings regarding the chapel. Two in particular had especially moved her.

One was from a man in Chicago who had just returned from a trip through the Southwest with his wife:

> On the day we visited, the Chapel was enjoying its usual, very substantial flow of visitors and I could not help but reflect on the importance of your part in providing the inspiration and the means for this lasting work of structural art. It expresses so well some of your own insights of spirit as it lifts the spirits and life-focus of so many people you will never meet...who are drawn to this master-work in its beautiful setting. Thank you again, from one who experiences this thrill on each returning visit. I might add that it did the same for my wife as she came upon it for the first time. In the several years since I shared the Chapel with several hundred friends through my Christmas cards with its picture, I have heard from many who did not know of it previously, but have visited it since...all coming away with a very real sense of being lifted in spirit by the experience. Cordially, Elmer H. Johnson.

Another letter was from a Canadian who described himself as a 'White Russian of the Greek Orthodox faith.'

> I never expected to be so touched, so deeply moved. I stood there and my tears were streaming, and I could not stop them...the beauty and simplicity of this finest architecture and surroundings. It is so marvelous, and I can only thank God I had the pleasure to be there. If God grants me health, I will return again, and I hope for more than one day. Thank you Mrs. Brunswig Staude for giving us people this great pleasure and possibility to share with you this beauty. Sincerely, Ben Tchavtchavadze.

Like a living presence, the Chapel of the Holy Cross rises like a shrine in the red rock splendor of Sedona. "It should not only be a monument to faith," said Marguerite several years before her death in 1988, "but a spiritual fortress..so charged with God, that it spurs man's spirit godward." And so it does.

Chapter Eight
THE MAN WHO MADE HIS DREAM COME TRUE
Abe Miller's Tlaquepaque

hat are you building here?" the woman
demanded. It was not the first time she
had sought out Abe Miller to ask that
question. Always before, he had shrugged
and replied, "I don't know yet." This
time he gave her a different answer.
"I think I'll build a hamburger stand. Is
that all right with you?"

Abe Miller kept people guessing for a year. No one knew for
certain what was being constructed beyond the adobe wall that lined
a four-and-a-half acre section of land along Highway 179. There
were no signs that announced the construction of anything.
People ventured past the wall out of curiosity. They could see
something remarkable was taking place, but what was it . . .
condominiums . . . townhouses?

The year was 1971 when Abe Miller, a prominent Nevada
businessman, had started construction of Tlaquepaque in the park-
like setting along the banks of Oak Creek. His first concern was
to preserve the trees and foliage that dominated this beautiful land.
Equally important was the style of the buildings. Abe wanted the
construction to be authentic colonial Mexican, built in the old world
manner. To achieve this, he took his architects and their construction crew on several trips into old Mexico so that they not
only learned the style, but captured the essence of what he was
trying to achieve. Tlaquepaque was to be a work of art where works
of art would be sold.

Miller spared no expense. He would not put a price tag on his
dream. He'd take his time and allow the dream to evolve slowly,
carefully and right. Only the best quality of workmanship was
tolerated. Authenticity must prevail over commercialism and
imitation. Above all, nature must be preserved. It took hundreds
of years for the graceful sycamores, cypress and other trees to grow
in this lovely setting. If the trees were in the way, Abe instructed
his architects to build around them. As a result, not one tree was
cut down.

His wife Lin recalled that the first building was the El Rincon Restaurant. It was constructed in order to show the men how to build Mexican-style, using irregular lines with thick walls. The light fixtures in El Rincon were made from authentic hand-carved oxen yokes, which Abe had brought back from Mexico.

Abe would fly into Mexico, rent a car, and go out where the real Mexican people lived. He'd tell the people what he was looking for. If it was iron work, they would lead him to a dump where piles of old iron work had been thrown away. Abe paid them for it, and then brought in trucks to haul it away. Most of it was painted white or pink, but Abe could see that it was hand-forged. He had to soak and soak them in acid baths to remove the paint. This iron work once had graced old homes and churches, and they were beautiful. The huge wooden door that stands in the entrance to the Patio where Rene's Restaurant is located comes from a 300 year-old church ruin in Mexico. The fountains and bells were flown in from either Mexico or Italy.

Abe learned his appreciation of quality, his shrewd business sense, his values of honesty and loyalty, and his modesty from his remarkable and highly successful father, John Franklin (J.F.) Miller.

From the time Abe was a little boy, his father, J.F. Miller's philosophy was: "Make a nickel look like a dollar, and save one cent back. You'll be amazed at how that penny will accumulate in ten years' time."

John Franklin Miller was the third oldest child in a Protestant family of nine children. His family was poor. When J.F. was a little boy, an uncle from California visited the family in Iowa and took a shine to J.F. He offered to raise him at his home in Solvang, California. The uncle owned a successful restaurant in Solvang. J.F. stuck with his uncle, learned the restaurant business and eventually bought a restaurant of his own in Solvang.

In later years, J.F. Miller climbed aboard a train and headed home to Iowa to pursue other adventures. He stepped off the train to stretch his legs in a dusty, insignificant little town called Las Vegas. There his journey ended.

The year was 1905, and on that fateful day the Union Pacific Railroad was holding a land auction. J.F. knew that with Los Angeles on one side and Salt Lake on the other, Las Vegas one day would have to grow, since it was the only real town and watering station in between. At that time, Las Vegas sported only two small hotels. The roads were not paved and there were no sidewalks, only boardwalks. With $2,000 and a hand-shake, J.F. Miller bought a parcel of land that is now on the corner of Main and Fremont Streets, and built the Nevada Hotel. Later he changed its name to the Sal Sagev Hotel (Las Vegas spelled backwards). He used only the finest materials inside and out. The Sal Sagev became a hotel which embodied quality ... the best of everything.

One of J.F.'s first employees was Rosa Marchetti, a lovely and brilliant young girl from Torino, Italy, whom he employed as a maid. After Rosa had worked at the Sal Sagev for several years, she took a vacation to New York to visit her sister and brother-in-law who were employed at the Ritz-Carleton Hotel. Rosa had been there only three days when a knock came at her door. It was J.F. "Rosa," he said, "I would like you to marry me." Rosa was taken aback. "John," she replied, "I need time to think about it." J.F. said he would return that afternoon. Rosa discussed the matter with her family and when J.F. returned, she said yes. The couple walked out into the streets of New York to find a Justice of the Peace to marry them. They went inside a home that had a sign outside which read: ABRAHAM COHEN - JUSTICE OF THE PEACE.

It was close to supper time when the Millers approached Mr. Cohen to perform the ceremony. Cohen's wife was in the midst of preparing homemade noodles for their supper. She stopped what she was doing to stand up for the Millers. Afterwards, the Cohens asked the Millers to stay and share supper with them. After the Millers left, J.F. turned to his bride and said, "Rosa, if we ever have a son, I want to name him Abraham after that kindly Jew." Thus their first child born on August 19, 1912, Abraham Paul Miller, got his name.

In later years when Abe applied to Northwestern University in Chicago and was accepted, he thought nothing of the fact that his father, who could well afford to send him to college, insisted that he pay his own way to school. Abe would work two years and attend college two years, then work two years and attend college again until he finally graduated in 1937. He still found time to play football, become captain of the football team, play basketball and run track. He was also active in a fraternity as well as other school functions.

Neither Abe nor his sister Helen, who became a brilliant businesswoman, ever resented the hard work or sacrifices their parents expected from them. That's how they were raised, and they respected their parents tremendously because of it.

While growing up, Abe and his sister, Helen, who deeply loved and respected one another, learned all phases of the hotel business. They performed every imaginable task from janitorial to working as front desk clerks. If Abe's bedroom in the hotel was needed for a late arriving guest, Abe was sent up on the roof to sleep. The family worked like an army of ants. They scraped together everything they had to create this fine hotel. J.F.'s profit after his first day of business was $1.50. That was what was left after paying all of his bills.

Later, according to Lin, J.F. ran a small bank in his hotel. When the Depression hit, he promptly paid off everyone who had money there except one. That's because J.F. never found the person. So he held on to the money for years, finally donating it to charity when it was never claimed.

The Sal Sagev Hotel catered to home town people. Widows from Los Angeles flew in each year and were always assured of the same room and fine service. In those days, no one had to worry about crime in the hotels. The restaurant the Millers started in their hotel served the best of everything. They started with real butter, and when they leased the hotel years later, (it's now called the Golden Gate Hotel and Casino) they were still serving real butter.

Linnea Sigred Christine Johnson of Los Angeles became the bride of Abraham Paul Miller on November 2, 1941, at the historic Mission Santa Inez in Solvang, California. Abe had met Lin two years before while he was a patient in a Los Angeles hospital. A lovely Scandinavian brunette, Lin Johnson had been Abe Miller's nurse.

"Abe had suffered an injury to his kidney while playing football at Northwestern," said Lin. "The injury was worse than the doctors originally thought. I attended him while he recovered from surgery."

A month after Lin and Abe were married, the Japanese bombed Pearl Harbor, and the United States prepared for World War II. The government installed Nellis Air Force Base in Las Vegas, and military personnel and their families arrived by the thousands. A building boom followed. The Millers had to set up cots in the hallways of the Sal Sagev Hotel in order to accommodate all of those people. According to Lin, Mother Miller's washing machine was going non-stop, filled most of the time with diapers.

That was the beginning of Vegas. There was no stopping it after that. Las Vegas would become known world-wide as having the best entertainment and the best food anywhere. Everyone who came to Vegas in those days also dressed elegantly.

During the war, whatever service clubs in town raised funds for the war effort, J.F. would match their funds. He asked only one thing in return . . . that his name not be mentioned for his generosity.

This was a very prosperous time for the Millers. Many people made money fast in those days, but most either lost it by gambling or making poor investments. Not J.F. He believed in progress, but he also believed in caution. It paid off.

J.F. Miller *sits in his buggy outside his Nevada Hotel, 1908*
Photo courtesy of Lin Miller

Las Vegas *after World War II. The Sal Sagev Hotel on the right as it looked around 1948. Photo courtesy of Lin Miller*

Abe Miller *All State Center, 1929*

Photos courtesy of Lin Miller

Rosa and J.F. Miller, *1910.*

In time, J.F. and Rosa chose to spend more of their time at their ranch in Kingman. J.F. had enough confidence in his two children, Abe and Helen, to leave them in charge of the hotel and all the other family businesses.

Rosa and J.F. were married 39 years before he died in 1957. He finally found in Rosa a woman he could trust, one who had an excellent business sense and who was always devoted and loyal. J.F. never could tolerate disloyalty nor phoniness. He was a man of very few words and he seldom smiled. But when he did smile, heaven opened up.

Lin added that J.F. was not a man to bear grudges, nor was Abe. "If either one came out on the short end of a deal, then they took their losses and learned from them."

John Franklin Miller lived until the age of 92. He watched his diet and walked straight as an arrow, according to Lin. He considered work a blessing and firmly believed everyone should pay their own way.

As long as the Sal Sagev Hotel was under the Millers, their employees remained loyal. It was not unusual for employees to work over a decade for the Miller family.

J.F. Miller also was an altruistic man who helped people out all over. Often they never knew where their help came from because he did it quietly. His son Abe would continue in this same tradition.

Helen and Abraham Miller, *1918*.
Photo courtesy of Lin Miller

The Abe Miller Family *1956.*
(left to right) Abe, Marilyn,
Lin, Carolyn and Paul
Photo courtesy of Lin Miller

Abe was the most kind man I ever knew. I was a Baptist and he a Catholic. It was never a problem between us. He attended my church and I attended (and was married in) his. When they built the West Charleston Baptist church in Las Vegas, I didn't learn until much later that Abe had provided money for flooring and roofing in the new church. He was not one to tell people, including his family, about the numerous charitable things he did.

Lin also described Abe's relationship with his father as close, and one dominated by respect. As for his relationship with his mother Rosa, that was a case of absolute adoration. Abe's feelings for Rosa were matched only by an equal adoration on her part for him.

As Las Vegas grew and grew, the Millers continued to prosper and invest in more enterprises, but the paper work soon became staggering. After his father died, Abe began to consider moving towards other opportunities.

Abe was a small town boy. When the government began dictating everything the Millers could or could not do with their own businesses; when the hotel was inundated with insufficient funds checks written by prominent people; and when Vegas became more of a "glitzy gulch" instead of the fine city he had grown up in, Abe realized he didn't want to live there anymore. So he began looking around for somewhere else to live.

Abe looked at several places, including Solvang, California, where his father was raised. He also looked in New Mexico and Arizona. He finally decided upon Sedona. Abe bought a cottage in Oak Creek Canyon, and later the Todd Lodge (now Garland's Lodge). For the next six years, he brought his growing family of three children (Marilyn, Carolyn and Paul), to spend the summers and holidays there.

Since Sedona was a place Abe and his family regularly visited, Abe soon became friends with Harry Girard. Girard owned a nursery on four-and-a-half acres of land near the banks of Oak Creek in the town of Sedona. After Harry put his land up for sale, he received several offers. When the prospective buyers described what they would do with the land, however, Girard hit the ceiling.

"They want to cut down all the trees and put in things like apartments," Girard told Abe. It made Girard furious. Before long, Abe started to consider buying Harry Girard's land. He wasn't sure at first what he might do with it, but he had an affinity for the property and a desire to work with God's creation. He knew that whatever he built there would not disturb the natural setting.

Finally an idea began to germinate, fed by Abe's long infatuation with the arts and architecture of colonial Mexico. Why not build a village of arts and crafts patterned after a lovely village Abe admired outside of Guadalajara, Mexico called Tlaquepaque, (ta-lock-a-pock-y)? The Indian interpretation of this word is "the best of everything."

When Abe told Girard about his idea, Girard was not impressed. He hated anything Mexican, preferring the Oriental instead. Girard joked that he would build a wall between his property and the portion he might sell to Abe, if that was what Abe was going to do.

If the sale went through, Girard planned to continue to live in his home (now the Kitchen Cottage) and work in his greenhouse (now the Atrium Restaurant). But Girard did love the fact that Abe promised not to destroy trees, and on that basis, a deal was finally struck.

In order to finance most of the project, Abe decided to sell other properties and concentrate on his own dream. Then he went to work, only it was never work to Abe. Tlaquepaque became the most delightful and enjoyable project Abe Miller had ever set his mind to.

After hiring the architects and a crew whom he flew into Mexico for research purposes, Abe hired Harry Girard as a

J.F. Miller *at 80 years old*
Photo courtesy of Lin Miller

Lin Miller with daughter, Marilyn,
1989. Photo by Kate Ruland-Thorne

consultant. Along with his wife, Lin, an accomplished and award-winning garden club member, the Millers took Harry on frequent trips to California to select plants and flowers that would flourish in Sedona's soil and climate.

As things began to come together, Girard had a change of heart. He told Abe he liked this elegant Mexican-colonial look after all. He withdrew his threat to build a wall.

But Abe began to notice that Girard was not himself. He was lying down much too often and didn't seem to feel good. Abe encouraged Girard to see a doctor, who told him he had an ulcer. Abe didn't buy it.

At his own expense, Abe flew Girard to his own doctor in Santa Barbara where tests showed that Harry Girard was seriously ill. He lived only three months more, never seeing the completion of Tlaquepaque. Later, Abe was able to purchase the remaining property where Harry's home and greenhouse were located.

Abe considered his earliest tenants in Tlaquepaque to be pioneers as much as he was. He helped out many struggling artists who wanted to work within its lovely setting, too.

Abe wanted Tlaquepaque to represent the "best of everything," including the most honorable and talented people. He built the upstairs of the buildings with the purpose of providing a place there for artists to live and work so they could sell their wares in the shops downstairs. But the artists complained that they never got any work done. People wanted to watch them work. So they decided it was best to work away from Tlaquepaque and Abe then turned the apartments into shops.

Photos by Kate Ruland-Thorne

*Three Hundred Year Old
Church Doors and
hand-forged iron gates
from Mexico.*

The Chapel at Tlaquepaque

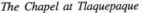

One of Abe's favorite buildings was the charming little chapel at Tlaquepaque. His friend, architect Ben Carpenter, said Abe was not a man to talk openly about God, he'd rather go into a church when it was empty and commune privately there. Abe often went into the little chapel at Tlaquepaque in the early mornings before anyone else was around.

As each phase of Tlaquepaque was completed, Abe assumed more and more responsibility for taking care of the grounds. Anyone trying to locate him would usually find him sweeping leaves, watering flowers or driving his tractor.

One of his greatest delights was to overhear comments from visitors who expressed astonishment over the loveliness of Tlaquepaque. On several occasions, people approached Abe while he was working and asked if he knew who had created Tlaquepaque. His answer was a shrug, as if he didn't know.

If I looked the world over, I could never have found a better husband, friend, or father for our three children, Paul, Carolyn and Marilyn. Abe encouraged me and shared my love for flowers and made many of the containers I used in flower shows which often earned me awards. Everyone wanted to know where I had found my containers and I would tell them Abe made them. When I won the national 'ARRANGER

Not a single tree was cut down.

Patios leading to patios.

Photos by Kate Ruland-Thorne

OF THE YEAR' award in 1982, I told everyone that half the award belonged to Abe because he had made the magnificent container.

Lin also saved many of the sweet notes Abe wrote to her and his children as they grew up. She shared one of her favorites, written at Christmas in 1977.

FOR MY LIN:
I've saved this expression for last (the good things come last) since I have just finished a short Yuletide note to our kids and told them I would try to be around if they needed me.
None of these good things would have materialized without such a truly wonderful, unselfish and concerning mother and wife. This my good fortune to have met you. Look at all the happy things that have happened to me.
My gift to you, my darling, is however I can say it with meaning --
However you found me, I am so lucky and everlastingly grateful --
All my love now, and on down the road.

Abe

On November 2, 1981, Lin and Abe celebrated their 40th wedding anniversary. By the following year, the final phase of Tlaquepaque was completed with the installation of an Italian fountain. The project had taken ten years.

That same spring, Lin became aware of an alarming change in Abe. She and Abe immediately flew to see their doctor in Santa Barbara who diagnosed Abe as having brain cancer. Three weeks after his surgery, Abe Miller died on March 30, 1982. Tlaquepaque had been completed just three months before.

News of Abe Miller's sudden death stunned all who knew him. Lin heard from numerous people, many she didn't know. A large number wrote to tell her how Abe had helped them in their time of need. Members of both the California and Colorado Garden Clubs wrote to say that trees had been planted in their states in his honor: a redwood in California and another tree at Denver's Botanical Gardens. The reason they gave was that Abe had helped many garden clubs nationwide create living testimonies to man's ability to work with nature.

Everyone agreed that Abe Miller's enthusuasm left a tremendous legacy of love, not only for his family and friends, but for all those who would ever visit Tlaquepaque.

Today, Tlaquepaque is the hub and heart of Sedona. Visitors from around the world continue to be awe-struck by Abe Miller's monument to beauty. Others have tried to duplicate Tlaquepaque but have fallen short. Perhaps they focused too much on costs or an eagerness to make money. Abe Miller succeeded because he concentrated on beauty.

Tlaquepaque was the culmination of a dream for this extraordinary man, and fortunately for Sedona, Arizona, he chose to make that dream a reality here.

Chapter Nine

HOLLYWOOD COMES TO SEDONA
Bob Bradshaw Remembers

egend has it that a 24-hour blizzard was all that kept Northern Arizona from becoming the film capital of the world. In 1913, a young Cecil B. DeMille was sent out west to make an epic pioneer film, "SQUAWMAN." It would be a make-or-break venture by the newly formed Jesse L. Lasky Feature Play Company. The location decided upon was Northern Arizona. But when DeMille arrived in Flagstaff with his train-load of technicians and actors, he was greeted by the worst snow storm in 50 years. Even though the storm cleared the following day, DeMille didn't wait for clear weather. He continued on west to California where he not only filmed SQUAWMAN, but founded Hollywood as well.

Silent film-making was already a thriving business in Prescott between 1912 to 1914. William Duncan's Selig- Polyscope Company had cranked out such pot-boilers as "HOW BETTY MADE GOOD," "MOUNTED OFFICER FLYNN," and "THE RUSTLER'S REFORMATION." Prescott also was the training ground for a young cowboy star named Tom Mix.

Jesse L. Lasky's Feature Play Company did return to Oak Creek Canyon to film Zane Grey's "CALL OF THE CANYON" in the 1920's. Grey had written the story while staying at the Lolomi Lodge (now gone) near West Fork. The silent film version of the story starred Richard Nix, Lois Wilson and Noah Berry. Instead of a snowstorm, the crew and stars found themselves stranded without food, supplies or indoor plumbing when a raging summer flood raised Oak Creek ten feet. After that, Hollywood forgot about Sedona and Oak Creek Canyon for awhile until the era of the 'Sagebrush Sagas' of the 30's. Then Hollywood's attitude changed as such films as "RIDERS OF THE PURPLE SAGE," "SMOKY," and "KING OF THE SIERRAS" were made here, convincing Hollywood at last that this was a prime area for film-making.

Since then, the list of stars who have been on location in Sedona and Oak Creek Canyon reads like the who's who of movieland's Golden era. They include Robert Young, Vaughn Monroe, Gene

Tierney, Robert Taylor, Randolph Scott, Barbara Bel Geddes, Robert Mitchum, Cornel Wilde, Lizabeth Scott, Maureen O'Hara, Gene Autry, Robert Preston, MacDonald Carey, John Payne, Ray Milland, Ward Bond, Tyrone Power, Dick Powell, Glenn Ford, Henry Fonda, Lee Marvin, Rock Hudson, Zachary Scott, Jimmy Stewart, Sterling Hayden, Joan Crawford, John Wayne, Elvis Presley and more recently, Linda Evans, Richard Chamberlain and Robert DeNiro. And this is only a partial list. That's because Hollywood has been coming to the Sedona area for over 60 years.

One fellow who has been involved with Hollywood's comings and goings for 40 of those 60 years is cowboy-carpenter-professional photographer, stunt man, bit player and location manager, Bob Bradshaw:

> I started working on the movies as a carpenter in 1946. I helped build the first western movie town over by Coffee Pot Rock for ANGEL AND THE BAD MAN which John Wayne produced and starred in. His co-star was Gail Russell. I helped build movie sets for ten years after that, which put me on the ground floor to work as a double, an extra or a bit player during shootings. Whenever the director or producer needed local extras, they'd have everyone file past them at the Sedona Lodge (now King's Ransom) and I never missed being picked for something. I was the right size to double actors who were usually six foot and skinny.

By 1956, Bradshaw was often called to find locations for movie companies as well, a task he continues to enjoy today. To date, he has worked on 16 television movies, 45 television commercials, 22 magazine ads, three videos and 26 feature films. He has rich memories and definite opinions about movies made then and today and about many of the stars mentioned above.

> Some of the first stars I doubled for were Lee Marvin and Rock Hudson in the movie GUN FURY. It was filmed here in the early fifties. There was one fight scene in that movie which was shot where the Chapel of the Holy Cross now stands. Rock Hudson had to fight a bad guy all up and down that hill. He didn't use a stunt man, he did the fighting himself. I heard the director, Raoul Walsh, say after the scene was finished that if (Gary) Cooper or (Gregory) Peck had tried that strenuous fight scene, they'd never been able to handle that hill.

Some of the great classic films shot in Sedona that Bradshaw worked on were JOHNNY GUITAR, BROKEN ARROW and THE ROUNDERS.

'ACE RANCHERO' *Bob Bradshaw has shoot-out on movie set near Coffee Pot Rock.*

'BROKEN ARROW' *Wagon train is attacked by Apaches near the Chapel of the Holy Cross.*

'BROKEN ARROW' *Two un-named extras wait for camera call during shooting of this movie.*

'SHOTGUN' *Bradshaw, who doubled for Zachary Scott, poses with the actor and his leading lady, Yvonne de Carlo.*

Photos courtesy of Bob Bradshaw

We made THE ROUNDERS in 1964. It starred Henry Fonda and Glenn Ford. Most of the filming was done out by Bell Rock. There wasn't anything built out there then. In fact the Village of Oak Creek wasn't there yet. The corral I helped build for that movie is still out there on private land. The guy who bought the land bought it while we were shooting the film.

Everyone who met Hank Fonda liked him. He was a real down to earth man. He'd rather hang around the locals than with the other stars or big wheels.

Fonda liked to drive his own car back and forth to the set. One day, the fellow who was supposed to watch the gate to the set didn't recognize Fonda when he drove up. This fellow asked, "who are you and what do you do on this film?" Fonda was real nice about it, even laughed. That fellow was sure embarrassed afterwards.

Casey Tibbs and Chill Wills also worked on THE ROUNDERS. Every night they'd head for uptown and proceed to get thrown out of every bar in town.

Tibbs was a World Champion rodeo rider and he doubled for Glenn Ford in all the bucking scenes. Boy could he ever ride. The director would tell him to buck over there and fall off over here. He'd fall off that horse right in front of the camera. It was really something. Tibbs came back to Sedona to double for Elvis Presley in STAY AWAY JOE.

When THE ROUNDERS producer, Richard Lyons, and his MGM staff were initially looking for a suitable location for their film, they traveled over much of Arizona, New Mexico and parts of California. They settled on Sedona for the same reasons most producers choose Sedona. "No where else did we find color quite as appealing as that of your red rock country," commented Lyons. "The sparkling color suits the mood of our film, which is a happy, hilarious modern western. It will be shown on wide-angle Panasonic because we don't want to miss any of this panoramic scenery."

It was this same panoramic scenery which drew Delmar Daves, director of BROKEN ARROW, to use Sedona locations. He had two film crews shooting at 30 different Sedona sites. Bradshaw and his crew constructed everything from wickiups for the hundreds of White River Apache Indians in the cast, to mangers for the horses, to giant plaster-of-Paris saguaro cacti which were set up from Cottonwood to Midgely Bridge to help these areas resemble Old Tucson.

Bradshaw was particularly impressed with how dedicated Daves was to authenticity in his epic true tale of ex-Army scout Tom Jeffords, (played by Jimmy Stewart), and his relationship with the great Apache leader Cochise, (portrayed by Jeff Chandler). Debra

'STAY AWAY JOE' *Bradshaw served as location manager for this film which starred Elvis Presley (standing to right of Bradshaw) and which was filmed almost entirely on Bradshaw's ranch.*

'JOHNNY GUITAR' *Joan Crawford and Sterling Hayden pose on set for Bradshaw who rode as an extra with the posse during filming.*

'GAMBLER II' *Linda Evans and Bruce Boxleitner pose for one of the last movies to be filmed on the Bradshaw ranch.*

'THE WILD ROVERS' *Ryan O'Neal helps William Holden rope a wild horse.*

'THE WILD ROVERS' *Bill Holden is dragged by a horse during filming at Hart Prairie near Flagstaff.*

Photos courtesy of Bob Bradshaw

Paget was the leading lady in that multi-million dollar film.

Of all the actors Bradshaw has worked with through the years, he says that Sterling Hayden was his favorite:

> Hayden was like Hank Fonda. He didn't act like a big shot movie star. He was just a regular guy without a big ego. I worked with him here on JOHNNY GUITAR, which also starred Joan Crawford and Mercedes McCambridge.
>
> Hayden came up to me one day and told me that Sedona was about the best location he'd ever been on...except for that bitch. He was referring to Crawford. That lady was on a real ego trip. I saw how mean she was to her kids. I offered to take all of the star's kids on a trail ride. She was the only one who refused to let her twelve-year-old son go. Boy was he upset. He probably would have had more fun than he'd ever had in his life, but no one could talk her into letting him go along with the rest of the kids. So I know all about that MOMMIE DEAREST stuff. Crawford drove everyone crazy on the set,too, particularly Mercedes McCambridge. Those two never stopped fighting, both on and off the screen.
>
> I also worked with Hayden on SHOTGUN. I doubled Zachary Scott in that movie. One night after we had finished shooting, we all climbed in a big stretch-out station wagon to go back to town. The director, the stars, the producer, the unit manager and the cameraman were all in the stretch-out. Hayden asked me what the director was paying me to work as a double. I said $25 a day, Hayden was furious and got all over him for paying me so little. Heck, I was glad to get that much in those days, but that was the kind of guy he was.

Bradshaw states that the requirements for being a location manager haven't changed much in 40 years. "You're still expected to know where everything is," he says. The fact that he has photographed every area between here and the Utah border for his extensive post card business has helped him know where the best locations are:

> Once it's clear to me what they want to film, I can visualize the scene and go directly to it within an hour or less. Others who call themselves location managers often drive the movie crew around for days and still can't find anything.
>
> Blake Edwards came here to film THE WILD ROVERS with Ryan O'Neal and William Holden. I had spent a week going over the locations with the unit manager, cameraman and producer. Blake came in the day before filming was scheduled and we showed him the locations previously found. One of the locations was the Bradshaw ranch. The scene to be shot the next day was one in which Holden ropes a horse

'INDIAN UPRISING' *George Montgomery stars in this film which was shot in and around the Chapel of the Holy Cross area long before there was a chapel or a subdivision.*

Photos courtesy of Bob Bradshaw

'FLAMING FEATHER' *The only movie that ever was allowed to be filmed at Montezuma Castle. It starred Sterling Hayden, Barbara Rush and Victor Jory.*

out of a wild herd. Blake agreed to start filming on my ranch the following morning. After we got back to the hotel, he changed his mind and decided instead to film in Flagstaff in the snow. These last minute changes are a unit manager's nightmare.

We all got in the helicopter the next morning and the first place I showed Edwards was a place on Hart Prairie. He liked it and that was where the scene was shot.

Two of the prettiest stars Bradshaw says he ever worked with are Rhonda Fleming and Yvonne DeCarlo:

Those blue eyes of Rhonda Fleming's would just about make you melt. I worked with her on THE REDHEAD AND THE COWBOY. Yvonne DeCarlo is a beautiful lady too. She was the leading lady in SHOTGUN. She ended up marrying the stuntman for that movie, Bob Morgan. Later he was ruined in the movie HOW THE WEST WAS WON. He had a bad accident on a logging car on a train. Someone chained the logs down wrong and when Bob was having a fight with another guy, the chain broke. A railroad iron went right through him. He lost his leg and his career as a stunt man was over after that. Yvonne stayed with him for a long time, but finally quit him. I guess he became a vegetable after that. I heard he drank too much.

Bradshaw doesn't approve much of the movies made today. He thinks it's stupid to put all those swear words in them:

Why do they have to use all those bad swear words? Hundreds of potential viewers, like kids and church people, are cut out when they do that. It's so unnecessary. When they filmed MIDNIGHT RUN here recently with Robert DeNiro, that movie had plenty of good action and a good story, but they ruined it, in my opinion, by filling the dialogue with so many cuss words.

I also get upset with some of the new directors nowadays. They seem to expect the public to figure out what the stories are about. I think they want us to read their minds about what they're trying to get across. That's sure not the way the directors did it in the old days. You always knew what was going on.

I thought LONESOME DOVE, which was recently shown on television, was a good example of how they used to make movies. That movie got high ratings because the script was good, it was clear what the director was trying to get across, it was realistic...you could tell the writer had done his homework, and the acting was excellent. I hope this means

'THE ROUNDERS'
*Stuntman Buzz Henry,
Casey Tibbs (back to
camera), Glen Ford and
Henry Fonda with camera
crew on set near Bell
Rock.*

'GUN FURY' *Badman Leo Gordon
poses with hero Rock Hudson during
filming. The movie also starred Lee
Marvin. Bradshaw doubled both
Marvin and Hudson.*

'CIMMERON STRIP' *Jack Elam,
Bradshaw and Henry Fonda relax
between scenes for the
popular 60's television series.*

'IMAGES OF INDIANS'
*The late Will Sampson
(left) narrated this
docudrama for PBS.
Filmed near Boynton
Canyon*

*Photos courtesy
of Bob Bradshaw*

they're going to start making more movies like that, since the public liked it so much. It was a real shot in the arm for Westerns.

Bradshaw, who likes to claim he's had two of the longest running businesses in Sedona, the post card business and the location business, is planning to build another movie set on his ranch. The last one was purposely burned down during the filming of a Wells Fargo television ad. He also continues to photograph anything and everything that might be of interest to the millions of tourists who visit our area.

Some of those tourists have been celebrities who have returned to make Sedona their home. To date, that list has included Orson Wells, Jane Russell, Dick Van Dyke and presently includes, James Gregory (who played the sarcastic detective on the long running T.V. series, BARNEY MILLER), Robert Shields (internationally acclaimed mime whose former partner is Lorraine Yarnell of Shields and Yarnell), the star of SUGAR BABIES and numerous other

'HALF-BREED'
Star Robert Young posed for Bradshaw near Sedona. Bradshaw doubled the star in the movie.

'LAST WAGON' *Felicia Farr with Tommy Rettig. Bradshaw doubled as a bad man in this movie.*

Photos courtesy of Bob Bradshaw

musical extravaganzas, Ann Miller, and well-known screen writer, novelist and character actor, Alan Caillou. So Hollywood not only comes to Sedona to make movies, sometimes it calls Sedona home.

In 1988, producer Arthur Loew said, "Arizona has all the advantages that the West Coast had 30 to 40 years ago. Its unspoiled and widely varied set of locations can be discovered within an hour's drive." This is especially true of Sedona and Northern Arizona. Veteran location manager Bob Bradshaw knows where the best locations are. He and the city of Sedona still continue to welcome film companies from around the world.

Bob Bradshaw currently is planning to produce four books. Three are related to movie-making in Sedona, and the other is a colored scenic book based on his photography of this area since 1946.

Although thousands of commercials and portions of major movies and television productions have been filmed in the Sedona area, the following is a list of those major motion pictures filmed in their entirety on location here.

Those marked with an asterisk are ones on which Bob Bradshaw worked, in one or more of his many capacities:

Call of the Canyon
Riders of the Purple Sage
Robber's Roost
Dude Ranger
Two In Revolt
Smoky
Texas Trail
Billy The Kid
Leave Her To Heaven
The Kingdom of the Spiders
Angel and the Badman*
California
Desert Fury
Gunfighters
Cheyenne
Albuquerque
Coroner Creek
Fabulous Texan
Station West*
Singing Guns
Tall In The Saddle
Blood On The Moon*
Broken Arrow*
Comanche Territory*
Copper Canyon*
Red Head and the Cowboy*
Indian Uprising*

Man in the Saddle
Hellfire
The Half-breed*
Flaming Feather*
Pony Soldier
Gun Fury*
Apache*
Strawberry Roan
Johnny Guitar*
Outlaw's Daughter
Drum Beat*
Shot Gun
Stranger On Horseback*
Last Wagon*
Last of the Duanes
3.10 To Yuma*
Yellowstone Kelly*
Legend of Lobo*
The Roundup*
Stay Away Joe*
Legend of the Boy Eagle
Firecreek*
Wild Rovers*
Survival*
Thunder Warrior*
Revenge of a Killer*

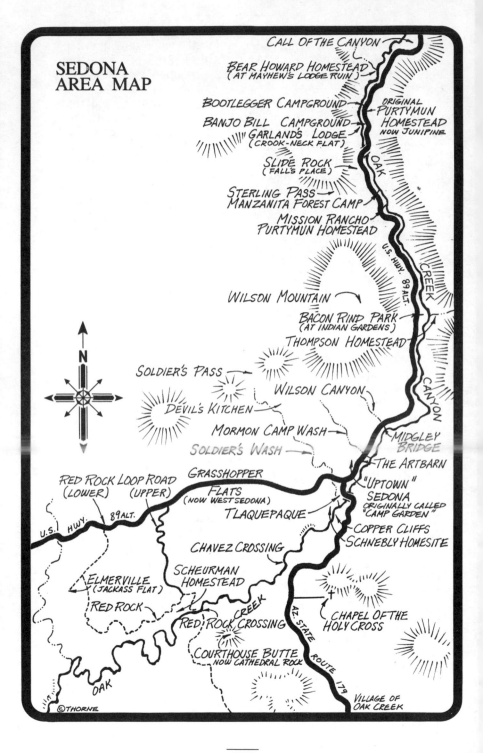

SEDONA
AREA MAP

CALL OF THE CANYON

BEAR HOWARD HOMESTEAD
(AT MAYHEW'S LODGE RUIN)

BOOTLEGGER CAMPGROUND

ORIGINAL
PURTYMUN
HOMESTEAD
NOW JUNIPINE

BANJO BILL CAMPGROUND
GARLAND'S LODGE
(CROOK-NECK FLAT)

SLIDE ROCK
(FALL'S PLACE)

STERLING PASS
MANZANITA FOREST CAMP

MISSION RANCHO
PURTYMUN HOMESTEAD

OAK

CREEK

U.S. HWY. 89 ALT.

WILSON MOUNTAIN

BACON RIND PARK
(AT INDIAN GARDENS)

THOMPSON HOMESTEAD

SOLDIER'S PASS

WILSON CANYON

DEVIL'S KITCHEN

MORMON CAMP WASH

SOLDIER'S WASH

CANYON

MIDGLEY
BRIDGE

THE ARTBARN

GRASSHOPPER

RED ROCK LOOP ROAD
(LOWER)   (UPPER)

FLATS
(NOW WEST SEDONA)

TLAQUEPAQUE

"UPTOWN"
SEDONA
ORIGINALLY CALLED
"CAMP GARDEN"

U.S. HWY. 89 ALT.

COPPER CLIFFS
SCHNEBLY HOMESITE

CHAVEZ CROSSING

ELMERVILLE
(JACKASS FLAT)

SCHEURMAN
HOMESTEAD

RED ROCK

CREEK

RED ROCK CROSSING

CHAPEL OF THE
HOLY CROSS

AZ STATE ROUTE 179

COURTHOUSE BUTTE
NOW CATHEDRAL ROCK

OAK

©THORNE

VILLAGE OF
OAK CREEK

Sedona Place Names

Garland's Lodge   Originally called Crook-neck Flat because of an old man with a crooked neck who camped there. In the 1890's, Bear Howard's son, Jess, built his cabin on the site, part of which is still enclosed in the lodge's kitchen. Bill Todd turned the place into a lodge in 1938. Later it was purchased by the Abe Miller family who sold it to the Garland family.

Stick-Leg Gulch   named for a man who fell into a century plant that stuck in his leg.

Sterling Pass   Named for a counterfeiter who hid out in the area and passed his counterfeit bills off in Jerome. He was captured after he left a trail of blood in the snow from a calf he had rustled and butchered.

Bootlegger Campground   Named for Bear Howard's grandson, Jess, who had stills there, and all up and down the canyon.

Bacon Rind Park   During Jerome's hey-dey, mining executives often camped in this place and fished. On one occasion they ran out of food except for a bacon rind. They tied a string to it and each one had a chew before it was yanked out of his mouth for the next person.

Soldier's Wash   Popular campground for cavalry soldiers from Camp Verde.

Soldier's Pass   Used by cavalry to track Apaches during the Indian Wars.

Grasshopper Flats   All of West Sedona was known by this name until after the turn-of-the-century. It had thousands of grasshoppers which fisherman caught on their way to Oak Creek.

Elmerville   Located near the present Kachina Riding Stables at Red Rock Crossing, named for an early settler who had changed its name from Jackass Flat. Jackass Flat was named for the wild burros that once roamed the area.

Mormon Camp Wash   Used as a campground by a Mormon family who was related to Grandma Thompson. The family stayed there each year on their way to their church stake in Mesa.

Camp Garden   Early name given Sedona by cavalry from Camp Verde who liked to cool off here in the summer.

Mission Rancho   Land owned by A.W. Purtymun between 1903-04 and then owned by Jess Purtymun from 1908 to 1923.

Slide Rock State Park   Originally owned by Harrington Fall and known as Fall's Place. Falls built a cabin there and a trail. It was purchased by Frank Pendley in 1907 who improved on the property and planted ochards.

Banjo Bill Campground   Named for banjo player Bill Dwyer who squatted there in 1880.

Wilson Mountain   Named for Richard Wilson who was killed by a bear there in 1885.

Manzanita Forest Camp   The only place in the canyon where a mining claim was ever filed. Later it was farmed as a forest lease by A.W. Purtymun.

Court House Butte   Now known as Cathedral Rock, one of the most photographed sites in Sedona. Its original name was given to it by Abraham James, Sedona's first settler and Grandma Thompson's father. He also is credited with naming Bell Rock, Steamboat Rock, Table Mountain and House Mountain.

Devil's Dining Room   A sink hole originally called Devil's kitchen until it caved in dramatically in 1880 filling the air with dust throughout the day.

SOURCES

Those Early Days Oldtimers' Memoirs by the Sedona Westerners,printed by the Verde Independent, 1975.

Arizona Highways "Oak Creek - Sedona Country Revisited," June, 1966.

The Inception and Construction of Schnebly Hill Road by Robert A. Novak - N.A.U. Special Collections Library.

Coconino County Supervisors' Minutes Vol. B-3 March 17, 1902 regarding the construction of Schnebly Hill Road.

Coconino Sun, Flagstaff "AGAINST STATEHOOD" - December 13, 1902.

Red Rock News "Beaverhead Stage Stop Commemorated," by Elizabeth Rigby - 1960.

Sedona Reflections Tales of Then For The Now by William Howard, Pronto Productions, Sedona, Arizona, 1982.

Red Rock News Special Edition "A Look At Sedona's Growth Through The Years", 1985, 1986, 1987.

Sedona Times Special Edition The Sedona Explorer, 1986.

The Verde Independent "A.E. Thompson Describes Early Sedona," Thursday, January 2, 1964.

Arizona - Arizona Days "The Story of Bear Howard," - Rosco G. Wilson, February 9, 1969.

The Dallas Morning News "Sedona, Arizona," Jean Simmons, June 15, 1986.

The Verde Independent "Those Were The Days," by Margaret Goddard, July 19, 1973; January 3, 1974.

An Old-Timer's Scrapbook A Roundup From The Range of His Own Recollections and Observations by Don Willard, Marker Graphics, Mesa, Arizona, 1984.

A Guide To Exploring Oak Creek and The Sedona Area by Steve Aitchison, RNM PRESS, Salt Lake City, Utah, 1989.

Oak Creek Canyon and The Red Rock Canyon Country of Arizona by Stewart W. Aitchison, Stillwater Canyon Press, Flagstaff, Arizona, 1978.

Plateau Magazine of the Museum of Northern Arizona "People of the Verde Valley," Vol. 53, No. 1, 1984.

Missouri Historical Society (pamphlet) "The History of Gorin, MO, 1966.

The Daily Gate City, Keokuk, Iowa "Gorin With Its Unique Name Has Civic Improvement In Mind," by Dorothy Pickett, September 15, 1962.

The Scotland County Public Library (pamphlet) "The Town of Gorin," from a taped interview with Gorin pioneer Mrs. Wallace Boyer.

"The History of Gorin," (pamphlet) by Gorin Pioneer Mrs. Ig Haff.

The Union Manchester, Boston, Mass., February 3, 1903 "How They Farm in a Big Canyon," by Harry Quimby.

The Schnebly Family Geneology Courtesy of Margaret Schnebly Wallace.

Correspondence from Ellsworth M. Schnebly to Southern Union Gas Company, Dallas - Western Savings Foresight, Phoenix - Sedona Westerners. N.A.U. Special Collections Library.

Sedona Magazine and Visitors' Guide "How Sedona Got Its Name," by Lisa Schnebly, Fall, 1986.

Arizona Highways "A Bell For Sedona," by R.J. Slade, May, 1959.

The Verde Independent "Sedona In Wonderland," by Harriet McIntosh, Elizabeth Rigby, May 21, 1964.

Westerner Getaway "Sedona: The Lady and Her Town," by Don Dedera.

Sedona Life "Schnebly Hill," by Heather Hughes, Vol. 1, No. 1, August, 1976.

Cowboy Artist: The Joe Beeler Story by Don Hedgpeth, Northland Press, Flagstaff, Arizona, 1979.

Doctor On Horseback by Ralph Palmer, M.D.

An Olgocene Colorado Plateau Edge by Damon and M. Shafigullah, Tectonophysics 61:1 - 24, 1979

Excavations at Three Sites in the Verde Valley by David A. Breternitz, Museum of Northern Arizona Bulletin 34, Flagstaff, 1960.

Hidden House, A Cliff Ruin in Sycamore Canyon by Keith A. Dixon, Museum of Northern Arizona Bulletin 29, 1956.

Two Ruins Recently Discovered in the Red Rock Country of Arizona by Jesse W. Fewkes, The American Anthropologist, 1896, Vol. 9, No. 8., pp. 263-283.

Verde Valley Archaeology Review and Prospective by Suzanne and Paul Fish, Museum of Northern Arizona, Research paper No. 4, Flagstaff, 1977.

Tuzigoot: An Archaeological Review by Dana Hartman, Museum of Northern Arizona Research Paper No. 4, 1976, Flagstaff.

The Hohokam, Sinagua, and The Hakataya by Albert H. Schroeder, Imperial Valley College Occassional Paper No. 3, 1979, Imperial Valley College Museum Society, El Centro, California.

Good Guys and Bad Changing Images of Soldier and Indian by Robert M. Utley, Journal of the Council on Abandoned Military Posts, 1976.

The Palatkwapi Trail Plateau Magazine of the Museum of Northern Arizona, Vol. 59, No. 4.

INTERVIEWS AND CORRESPONDENCE

Marguerite Brunswig Staude, August 1986

Tony Staude, July, 1989

Margaret Schnebly Wallace (daughter of Carl and Sedona Schnebly), February through July, 1989

Clara Schnebly McBride (daughter of Carl and Sedona Schnebly), February through July, 1989

Paula Schnebly Hokanson, April 1989

Clement Miller, Gorin, MO, Oct 1988

Gertrude Schnebly Stalworthy, April 1989

Linneah Miller (Abe Miller's wife), June through July, 1989

Marilyn and Carolyn Miller (Abe Miller's daughters), Summer, 1986

Laura Purtymun McBride, May through July, 1989

Joe and Sharon Beeler, July, 1989

Nassan Gobran, February and June, 1989

Bob Bradshaw, June, 1989

Callie Smith, Scotland County Historian, March, 1989

Warren Cremer, Time Expeditions Tours

Peter Pilles, Coconino National Forest

Fred Spinks

Quentin Durell

Assorted spirits and ghosts

INDEX

Miller, Abe, 87, 90, 91, 92, 93, 94, 96, 98
Miller, Ann, 109
Miller, Lin, 88, 90, 91, 92, 98
Miller, J.F., 88, 90, 91, 92
Miller, Helen, 91
Miller, Carolyn 96
Miller, Marilyn, 96
Miller, Paul, 96
Miller, Amanda, 42, 55
Miller, Philip, 41, 42, 43, 44, 45, 52
Miller, Sedona, 42, 43, 44
Miller, Lilly Victoria, 44
Miller, Pearl, 52
Mingus Mountain, 29, 39
"Midnight Run," 106
Modigliani, 77
Mogollon Rim, 6
Montana Historical Society, 71, 73
Montezuma Castle, 8, 10, 13
Montezuma Well, 2, 10, 13
Mormon Camp Wash, 30
Monroe, Vaughn, 99
Munds Park, 18, 47
Munds Springs, 22
Navajo, 2, 10
Nail, Frank, 24
Nail, Myrtle, 24
Nail, Ivy, 24
Nail, Maggie, 24
Nestler, Al, 66, 71
Nellis Air Force Base, 90
Nevada Hotel, 88
Nicholson, Marilyn, 66, 67
Nix, Richard, 99
Oak Creek Tavern, 72
O'Brians Art Emporium, 69
Octavia, Missouri, 42
Old Oraibi, 4
Old Pinal, 38
Onate, Juan de, 10
O'Neal, Ryan, 104
Owenby, Frank, 45

Padget, Debra, 104
Palatki, 1, 9
Palatkwapi, 4, 6
Palmer, Dr. Ralph, 50
Papago, 13
Peck, Gregory, 100
Phippin, George, 71, 72, 73
Phoenix Art Museum, 74
Phoenix, Arizona, 17
Pilles, Peter, 3, 6
Pima, 13
Pony Express, 34
Prescott, Arizona, 17, 18, 47
Presley, Elvis, 101
Purtymun, Albert, 22, 24, 38, 39
Purtymun, Charley, 22, 24, 38
Purtymun, Clara, 24, 39
Purtymun, Dan, 22, 38
Purtymun, Della, 24, 26
Purtymun, Elsie, 24
Purtymun, Emery, 38
Purtymun, George, 38
Purtymun, Ida, 22, 38
Purtymun, Jess, 22, 24
Purtymun, Laura, 24, 26, 30
Purtymun, Lizzie, 24
Purtymun, Mattie, 20, 29, 39
Purtymun, Pearl, 38, 39
Purtymun, Ruby, 38
Purtymun, Steve, 20, 29, 38, 39
Purtymun, Violet, 24
Purtymun, Virginia, 24
Purtymun, Zola, 24
Red Rock School, 29
Remington, Frederick, 72
Rene's Restaurant, 88
"Riders of the Purple Sage," 99
Rigby, Elizabeth, 63
Rigby, Douglas, 63
Rio Verde Reservation, 10, 12
Ritz-Carlton Hotel, 89
Rockefeller Center, 79
Rouat, 81
Russell, Gail, 100

How to Order Other Thorne Enterprises Publications

Experience Sedona Recreational Map.................................$4.95
"With the help of a new map called EXPERIENCE SEDONA, we explore red rock trails, the Mogollon Rim and vortex areas such as Boynton Canyon, touted for having psychic energy of the levels attributed to Stonehenge and the Pyramids of Egypt. I kept this map in my car along with my map of Italy."
Judith Morgan - The Los Angeles Times

Experience Sedona Legends & Legacies................................$8.95
by Kate Ruland-Thorne
A pioneer history of Sedona. "More delightful than her accurate, specific information, is her choice of topics and her method of presenting them."
Lois Stalvey Sedona Red Rock News

The Yavapi, People of the Red Rocks....................................$6.95
by Kate Ruland-Thorne
Told from their point of view: "The tribe has for many years had the desire to have this (book) accomplished. Now that it has been completed, I commend Kate Ruland-Thorne for a job well done."
Lois Hood - Planning coordinator for Ft. McDowell Mohave- Apache Indian Community.

White Eyes, Long Knives & Renegade Indians............................$5.95
by V. Keith Thorne
"A well researched and fascinating account of General Cook's campaign against the Tonto Apache and Yavapai Indians."
Col. Richard Norman -U.S. Army, Retired

The Legacy of Sedona Schnebly....................................$5.95
by Kate Ruland-Thorne
"I am grateful for the careful research and creative talent that led to Kate Ruland-Thorne's vivid and accurate portrayal of my great grandmother, Sedona Schnebly. Renderings such as hers keep alive the spirit of the woman."
Lisa Schnebly Heidinger

Experience Jerome $6.95
by Nancy Smith and Jeanette Rodda
"Experience Jerome is a professionally Written book that tells how a fascinating area got to be fascinating."
James Cook, Arizona Republic

Screw The Golden Years $6.95
I'd rather live in the past
by V. Keith Thorne
A humorous look at growing old.

Screw The Golden Years - Book 2 ....$6.95
Oh the joys of getting old
by V. Keith Thorne
A sequel, which is even funnier than the first.

Order Form

Customer				
Address	City	State	Zip	
Phone		Date Ordered		

DESCRIPTION	QUANTITY	PRICE	P & H	TOTAL
Experience Sedona Recreational Map		$4.95	$1.75	
Experience Sedona Legends & Legacies		$8.95	$1.75	
The Yavapi, People of the Red Rocks		$6.95	$1.75	
White Eyes, Long Knives & Renegade Indians		$5.95	$1.75	
The Legacy of Sedona Schnebly		$5.95	$1.75	
Experience Jerome		$6.95	$1.75	
Screw The Golden Years		$6.95	$1.75	
Screw The Golden Years - Book 2		$6.95	$1.75	

(Checks or Money Orders Only) Tax 8.5% for Arizona Residents only.
Mail to: Thorne Enterprises Publications
c/o Sedona Books & Music
140 Coffeepot Rd, Ste E-103-A
Sedona, AZ 86336
(Add $ .50 to each additional copy for postage and handling).

SUB-TOTAL	
TAX	
TOTAL	